JAPANESE DESIGN

• PENNY SPARKE •

Japanese Design

• MICHAEL JOSEPH •

For Molly

First published in Great Britain by Michael Joseph Ltd
27 Wrights Lane, London W8
1987

British Library Cataloguing in Publication Data

Sparke, Penny
    Japanese design.
    1. Design — Japan
    I. Title
    745.4′4952   NK1484.A1

    ISBN 0-7181-2875-3

Conceived and produced by Swallow Publishing Ltd
Swallow House
11-21 Northdown Street
London N1 9BN

Editor   Anne Yelland
Art director   Elaine Partington
Designer   John Meek
Picture researchers   Anne-Marie Ehrlich,
Sian Evans, William R. Tingey
Editorial consultant   Bruce Bentz
Studio   Del and Co

Typeset by Ampersand Typesetting Ltd, Bournemouth
Origination, printing and binding in Hong Kong
by Imago Publishing

Previous page: Shopping bag designed by
Shozo Kakutani for Yamaya Co. Ltd, 1985.
Above: Craftsmen at work in the Nogawa establishment, Kyoto.
Opposite: Ghost chair, designed by Keijiro Odera, 1986.

• Contents •

Introduction

'Our aesthetic sense is our order'[1]

The upward slants on the curves on roofs, such as on the 'torii' gate at the Itsukushima shrine at Miyajima, are one of the features of traditional Japanese aesthetics which have influenced contemporary Japanese design – from architecture to automobiles.

For many people, the term 'Japanese design' evokes the high level of aesthetic achievement of the country's traditional applied arts, from ceramics to lacquerwork to architecture. For others, it is associated with the strong visual appeal of the consumer gadgets that pour out of Japan's new, post-war production centres. These two parallel, and seemingly divergent, aspects make the concept of Japanese design difficult to define.

The inherent problem in trying to discuss these two aspects of Japanese design in a single breath is that they function within different cultural and historical contexts and on different cultural levels. The former depends on the continued close link, within traditional Japanese culture, between aesthetics, religious belief and everyday life. The latter is a spin-off from Japan's highly successful efforts to mass-produce, with imported technology, a wide range of technically innovative goods – cameras, audio and video equipment, domestic appliances, motorcycles and cars – which will compete in world markets on the bases of low cost and high technical efficiency. The appearance of these products, while undoubtedly fascinating and novel to many foreign customers, was, in the early post-war years at least, less a result of a specific visual policy on the part of the manufacturers than of technological and economic expediency combined with an eye to the preferences of foreign markets.

Although at first sight there is no common ground between these two views of Japanese design, they can be discussed together. This is because, in spite of so much Western influence and hybridization within Japanese culture in this century, many traditional Japanese aesthetic concepts have carried through into the present, providing a link with the past and a strong sense of cultural continuity. As J. V. Earle has written, 'Modern Japan is a unique example of the way in which a sophisticated urban culture has adopted Western methods to take on and outstrip the West in terms of trade, industry and the like and yet, to a remarkable degree, has retained its distinctive character.'[2]

While this continuity is very easily observed within contemporary Japanese everyday life – in, for instance, the way traditional food is presented and small parcels are wrapped – and within those contemporary Japanese design areas in which the individual plays a strong part – architecture, fashion, graphics and craft, for example – it is less easily discerned in high-technology products. In mass-production industries, the designer is an anonymous team member within a large corporation, and design is part of a very complex formula which includes marketing and sales. Even there, however, the persistence and ubiquity of cultural values have meant that many traditional Japanese aesthetic concerns *have*

An immaculate way of wrapping items has, for centuries, represented one of Japan's aesthetic strengths. These 'chimaki', or rice dumplings wrapped in bamboo leaves, demonstrate how attention to packaging detail extends to the preparation of food.

Left: This suit of Japanese armour from the nineteenth century, based on a fourteenth-century model, shows clearly how one aspect of traditional Japanese visual culture favours complexity and attention to minute detail.

In contrast to the visual detail on the suit of armour, the aesthetic impact of the stepping stones in the garden of the Knochiin Nanzenji Temple in Kyoto derives from their stark simplicity and closeness to nature.

survived and flourished – among them, miniaturization and portability, multi-functionality, attention to minute detail rather than to overall form, and the decorative use of functional components. In addition, a few high-technology companies, such as Honda, Yamaha and Sony, have made deliberate attempts to define design policies which take into account many well-established aesthetic concepts. It is clearly more difficult to sustain traditional values in areas which depend upon imported technology and the use of new, unfamiliar materials. None the less, there are increasing signs that Japanese industry is anxious to do so. This account of Japanese design, while trying to avoid a preoccupation with issues of 'good' and 'bad', will therefore focus on the conscious efforts that have been made since the Second World War to evolve a national design movement which takes into account Japan's past achievements, and which, in turn, forms the basis of a growing international design movement.

Ironically, many of its characteristics have not been taken directly from an appreciation of traditional aesthetics, but at second hand through the intervention of the European and American Modern Movement. What may seem like the influence of Western culture on Japan from the 1930s onwards is really just another means of Japan's realigning itself with its own traditional culture in an international context. For the Modern Movement depends considerably upon essentially Japanese principles, although this has been largely overlooked, and one of the aims of this book is to redress that imbalance and to suggest how central Japan's influence was to the aesthetic assumptions that underpinned the international architecture and design movement. As Robin Boyd has explained, 'Many qualities in the Japanese tradition match emotionally the most advanced mood of international architecture. These include the love of naked materials, the delight in open space at the expense of partitions and furnishing impedimenta, the pleasure of demonstrating the structural means of support and the satisfaction in the use of a module.'[3] Japan's obsession, through the 1950s, with the Western Modern Movement of the pre-war years was, in fact, not just in answer to the need to address an international market, but also a means of its looking at its own traditions at one remove and thereby coming to terms with them once again.

To say that contemporary Japanese design still depends upon traditional aesthetics is not, however, to imply that there is only one 'style' visible today. For several centuries, Japan has been able to accommodate two highly contrasting styles, the one, in the words of J. V. Earle, 'colourful, decorative, exuberant and inventive'[4] and the other 'monochrome, linear, refined and austere'.[5] Japan is a country of constant dualisms, of, for example, the co-existence of Western and Eastern ideas, and of decoration and austerity. As Masaru Katsumie explains, 'They turn eclecticism to their advantage and use it as a means of adding variety and enjoyment to their lives.'[6]

The main reasons for the existence of this overt eclecticism within Japanese culture can be found in the way it accumulates and retains

In the eighteenth and nineteenth centuries in Japan the wood-block or 'ukiyo-e' print was a cheap form of expendable mass culture, much-loved by the members of the new merchant class. This colourful example, by Sadahide, is entitled 'Foreigners in Yokohama'.

cultural values rather than letting one replace another. For example, when Buddhism was introduced into Japan, it left room for Shintoism, and today there is as much evidence of the presence of, say, sixteenth-century Buddhist culture in Japan as there is of eighteenth-century Japanese merchant culture or twentieth-century European culture. Having always taken from abroad, Japan is used to absorbing foreign influences and making them its own: there is a time and a place within Japanese culture for each one. The fundamental Japanese belief in the changes brought about by the cycle of the seasons encourages its highly flexible attitude towards cultural variance.

As there is so much of Japan's cultural past in its cultural present it is important to understand where some of the basic aesthetic tenets originate. The most important reason, however, why these aesthetic traditions are still relevant to contemporary culture is the fact that they have always been based on 'popular' rather than 'aristocratic' values. As such, they have influenced the life-styles of the vast majority of the Japanese population, so that it is possible to talk realistically about 'shared values' and 'known rules' in a way that is difficult to do in the West where aesthetic codes have not moved freely through class barriers. The highly controlled and homogeneous nature of Japanese society, and the traditional emphasis upon the social group, rather than upon the individual, have enhanced this respect for rules and allowed them to flourish as a means of reinforcing group activity and stability.

The strongest influence upon Japan's traditional aesthetic values has been that of Buddhism. Introduced from China in the sixth century, Buddhism joined Shintoism to become one of the two most influential religions in Japan. Buddhism brought with it a more philosophical approach to life than Shintoism, and a strong link between aesthetics and morality underpinned the Buddhist creed. Buddhist monks organized their lives in their monasteries on the idea of the 'economy of means'. According to Buddhist belief, poverty, austerity and simplicity were a means to contemplation and spirituality. These ideals provided the philosophical framework for the famous Japanese ritual tea-ceremony, or 'Cha-No-Yu'. It established a number of important aesthetic rules which are still the basis of the Japanese life-style and which, according to A. L. Sadler and C. E. Tuttle, 'have kept the national taste more sensitive and healthy and potent than that of perhaps any other country'.[7]

Originally imported from China, tea-drinking was turned into a specifically Japanese ceremony at around the end of the fourteenth century by Murata Shuko who advocated its introduction into private homes as well as in the special tea-rooms within monasteries. 'Teism', as it became called, was transformed, however, in the sixteenth century by Sen Rikyu, the greatest tea-master of all, into the ritual that it remains today.

There are several important aspects of the tea-ceremony which concern the establishment of an aesthetic code of behaviour. They include the use of only a precise number of utensils needed for the task – among them a 'furo' or furnace, a 'gotoku' or trivet, a ladle and charcoal tongs, a slop bowl, a 'mizu-sashi' or water-vessel, a kettle and kettle-stand, tea-caddies, and ceramic tea-bowls. A lack of decoration or ostentation in these utensils, a standardized, ritualized behaviour involved in preparing and taking tea, and the ultimate emphasis on the spiritual aspect of the action rather than the material end are also vital elements of the ritual.

A number of Japanese terms evolved in connection with the tea-ceremony which were used to describe the aesthetic elements within it: 'wabi', for example. This is a general concept which has been translated in a number of different and rather confusing ways. It is used, in the general sense, to mean 'a way of life synonymous with poverty and limitation'[8] and implies the 'attainment of spirituality without material possession'.[9] It

The East Pagoda of the Yakushiji Temple in Nara, one of the oldest Buddhist temples in Japan. Buddhist culture was introduced into Japan in the sixth and seventh centuries during the Nara period, joining Shintoism as one of the country's dominant religions.

The concept of 'shibui' or 'astringency in taste' is well exemplified in the simple, rustic aesthetic of these ceramic cups used in the tea-ceremony. The irregular decoration on their surfaces and their 'unfinished' forms seem to have occurred almost by chance.

further suggests the idea of 'imperfection' or 'irregularity' which comes from living one's life in direct contact with the rawness of nature. As an aesthetic concept the notion of 'rusticity' has remained fundamental to much of the work produced by Japanese craftsmen, particularly potters, over the years.

An accompanying, and more specifically aesthetic concept to 'wabi' is that of 'sabi' which has been at the centre of a great deal of discussion about Japanese art and design over the centuries, particularly in relation to the European Modern Movement. It refers, specifically, to the timelessness, simplicity, and purity of Japanese objects, but also to the idea that if an object functions well then it must look good. The aesthetic of economy that emerges from these concepts is at the heart of the Japanese approach to everyday life, not just of the tea-ceremony, and permeates numerous areas of contemporary Japanese design.

'Shibui', which emerges constantly in this context, derives from the specifically Zen-Buddhist concept of expressing spirituality through minimal aesthetic means. A good example is the highly rigorous Zen approach to garden design where two stones placed strategically can stand for the whole universe. 'Shibui', meaning literally 'astringency in taste',

The 'Cha-No-Yu', or tea-ceremony, has been practised in Japan in its present form for about four hundred years. Both a social and spiritual ritual, it is highly stylized and depends upon minimal surroundings and the use of the correct set of utensils.

This eighteenth-century cup, with an image of Mount Fuji on its side, is used in the tea-ceremony.

The interior of a villa used as living quarters by the wife of a feudal lord of Kishu, showing the use of 'shoji', or movable screens. These examples by Yasunobu Kano are painted with landscapes depicting the four seasons.

refers to this frugal use of material means for spiritual ends. In the Buddhist code of behaviour and, as a result, for the majority of the Japanese population, a life of simplicity and lack of ostentation was thought to be the only acceptable one. Conspicuous display was frowned upon. What decorative effects there were in objects were derived simply from the materials used – wood, bamboo, lacquer, clay and so on – rather than from any additions. In this way, the materials themselves, and the way they are used, become crucial and are highlighted (the so-called 'economy of means'). A set of taste values developed from these beliefs which, for many centuries, influenced the look of many accoutrements of Japanese life.

The traditional Japanese house, for example – the setting for, among other events, the tea-ceremony and therefore seen as an extension of that ritual – manifests many aspects of 'shibui'. As such, it has acted over the years as the forcing ground for many of the components of the aesthetic code that the Japanese adhere to so carefully. Made of wooden beams and constructed with a 'pillar and beam' method, which symbolizes the temporary shelter provided by the outstretched branch of a tree, the Japanese house is, traditionally, a small, simple space with a minimal amount of low storage furniture within it. The floor area where eating and sleeping take place is emphasized. Movable paper screens, called 'shoji', separate spaces from each other and provide a flexibility and openness within the space which is always multifunctional and kept clear of any unnecessary objects. The only extra decoration is provided by a selection of carefully arranged small objects exhibited in an alcove or 'tokonoma'. These are changed according to the season and, when not in use, are stored – as are the bedding, clothing, and culinary utensils – well out of sight.

The aesthetic rules that have emerged over the centuries from this rigorous, highly regulated way of living in such a confined space include an emphasis on compactness, portability, rectilinearity, selectivity and minimalism – all of which feed directly into the contemporary Japanese material environment.

One of the most imporant features of the Japanese house is an emphasis on modularity which stems from the use of multiple 'tatami' floor mats – each one measuring six feet by three feet. The size of each room is described by the number of mats contained within it. In turn, the size and proportions of the house itself are determined by the repetition of this module in the wall panels. This emphasis in Japanese living of focusing on the single unit first, and then on the outer shell, has created a very particular Japanese way of understanding form which operates by moving from the inside to the outside, from the detail to the whole, from the microscopic to the macroscopic. This way of seeing and perceiving has direct significance for such multi-component objects as hi-fi equipment and automobiles. It means that the control knobs of the hi-fi and the chrome trim on the side of the car door panel are the starting points for an aesthetic appreciation of the objects, not the metal box which houses them. Westerners, on the other

A Japanese serving-bottle showing clearly the way in which the decoration of so many traditional Japanese objects derives solely from the natural qualities of the materials used – in this instance clay and natural glazes.

hand, tend to look at the form first, rather than the detail. Inevitably this fundamental difference in perception has caused misunderstandings between East and West and makes it difficult for Westerners to see many Japanese designs as the Japanese see them.

The Japanese emphasis upon the particular as a symbol of the general, on the unit as a base for repetition, and on the sparing use of objects, was of enormous significance for protagonists of the Modern Movement. They saw, within Japanese culture, the possibility of a new aesthetic which they felt would be sympathetic to the concept of standardization that was emerging from the techniques of mass production. What they ignored, however, were the equally important ideas in Japan about the importance of materials, of craftsmanship and, above all, of the spiritual and moral context for these aesthetic rules.

A two-fold screen, from the latter half of the seventeenth century. Richly decorated objects like this became very popular in the West in the second half of the nineteenth century.

The concept of standardization extends in Japan beyond architecture, to dress for example. The kimono is also made of modular units, so that for centuries everyone has been able to make their own clothes in their own homes. Decoration is also important in this context. Its role in traditional Japanese design is very symbolic. The rules of colour symbolism are highly structured – only children and young people are, for instance, allowed to wear bright colours – and pattern, always derived from nature but stylized in a flat graphic manner, is also used for more than mere decoration. In the kimono, it is used both for variety – to counteract the strictness and uniformity of the garment's shape and proportions – and to enhance the areas of greatest attractiveness in women, such as the back of the neck.

An increased use of decoration and colour originated during the Edo period (1602-1867) when the merchant classes started to become powerful.

A lacquer screen with a sun and sea design, from the seventeenth or eighteenth century; this type of decorative item represents the kind of Oriental design sought by the Western world. The flat stylization of natural imagery is typically Japanese.

They developed a number of highly flamboyant, ostentatious and exuberant art forms, among them the kabuki theatre and the ukiyo-e wood-block print, which aptly expressed their essentially 'bourgeois' values. Although the materialism associated with these forms contrasts sharply with the widespread asceticism of Japanese life, they have become an important aspect of the twentieth-century Japanese aesthetic, expressed in today's urban environment by, for example, the cacophony of graphic signs and the highly complex 'technology' look of so many contemporary electronic gadgets.

The 260 years of the Edo period, which ended after Japan opened her doors to the West in the 1850s, had two important effects for subsequent Japanese cultural developments. The first, achieved through the strict control of the life-style of the majority of the Japanese population, and the ban on contact with any alien cultures, was the careful preservation of all the traditional aesthetic rules that had evolved up until that time. The second was its encouragement of a new highly flamboyant style. When Westerners first gained access to Japanese culture, this flamboyance characterized the objects – the fans, kimonos, lacquerwork, prints and other luxury items – made available to them, and suited their own 'bourgeois' aspirations.

In the late twentieth century both the austere and the exuberant strands of Japanese design are, in the words of J. V. Earle, 'very much alive and well in modern Japan'.[10] The austere is expressed in the many vestiges of traditional culture; the exuberant in the more popular aspects of contemporary Japanese urban life, such as noisy 'pachinko' halls, garish love hotels, and vulgar comic-books and crude mechanical toys.

There is a danger, however, in trying to document the aesthetic similarities between contemporary Japanese artefacts and those from the traditions of the past; it is easy to forget that their conditions of conception and manufacture are very different. The creation, for example, of a ceramic tea-bowl in the best traditions of the Japanese tea-ceremony is hard to compare with the production of a highly technical, multi-component object, such as an electronic calculator which has been designed by a team, manufactured by automated technology and marketed in Europe and the USA. Beyond their shared compactness and portability they exist, to a large extent, in different worlds. Nevertheless the comparison is valid, and this book sets out to answer the provocative question: what happened to traditional Japanese aesthetic concepts when they were confronted with high technology, new materials and international marketing? It will focus, therefore, on the evolution of Japanese design, across a wide range of media, in the period from the 1860s to the present day. By looking at the nature and significance of many of the objects that have emerged, it will examine both the ideology behind many recent design decisions and the structure within which they have been made. In the process, a new insight into the elusive concept of 'Japanese design' will become apparent.

A neon-lit 'pachinko' hall where Japanese men spend hours playing pinball machines – another instance of the more garish, popular end of the contemporary Japanese urban scene.

Far left: A street scene in contemporary Tokyo depicts the rich mixture of different graphic signs typical of the post-war Japanese urban environment.
Left: A love hotel in Tokyo – a much-needed retreat for courting couples and an example of Japanese architectural 'kitsch' at its most extreme.

PART ONE
Chapter 1

Prosperity, strength and culture:
1860-1940

The story of Japan, from the 1860s up to the eve of its involvement in the Second World War, is dominated by both its impact on the West (in terms of its influence on the Modern Movement in painting, architecture and design), and by its borrowing from the West in the areas of modern technology and industry. Although at the turn of the century the West tended to see Japan as a rather primitive country, in spite of its highly developed aesthetic sensibility, Japan was, in fact, dramatically transforming itself into one of the world's leading industrial powers.

Modern Japan took the first steps towards becoming a highly sophisticated industrial nation soon after it opened its doors to trade with the USA and Europe in the 1850s. For more than 250 years it had experienced a period of total isolation under the rule of the Tokugawa shoguns, during which, although steady and significant domestic commercial progress had taken place, no foreign trading had been permitted. Japan had reaped no advantages from the scientific, technological and industrial breakthroughs made in Europe at that time and, politically, the country was still dominated by a feudal system which had changed little for two and a half centuries. However, in the area of handicrafts, regional specializations had developed and national markets were established. Traditional Japanese aesthetic ideals were maintained in these years of stasis, although a new and uncharacteristic flamboyance also emerged in the new art forms which flourished with the rise of the merchant class in this period.

The years of isolation served, therefore, to consolidate Japan's traditional areas of production but there was little development in the 'new' industries – in shipbuilding, for example, mechanized textile production, and metal fabrication. In the 1850s, when the acceleration of international trading and the coming of steamships caused Europe and America to entreat Japan to open its doors to them, all this was to change. Between 1854 – the year in which the American Commodore Perry signed a trade agreement with Japan – and 1868 – the year of the so-called 'Meiji Restoration', when the shoguns handed over power to the Emperor – the preconditions for change were laid down. As a symbol of what was to come, on the occasion of its trade agreement, America presented Japan with a model locomotive, an electric telegraph and a daguerrotype camera.

This Japanese wood-block print is entitled 'Foreigners at Namamugi near Yokohama being attacked and killed'. The Japanese distrust of foreigners before the Meiji period was so strong that they were not allowed in the country.

A wood-block print, from
the nineteenth century, by
Yoshitoshi. This shows the
arrival of Commodore
Perry in Japan – the first
moment of major contact
between Japan and the
West for over two hundred
years and a turning point in
modern Japanese history.

In Japan, the 1870s and 1880s were decades of intense modernization and, above all, of almost fanatical Westernization. Western dress and interiors were introduced as a result of the dissemination of images from the West. They were, in the words of Yoshida Mitsukuni, 'symbols of progress. . . . It naturally became the norm that the higher a person stood in the élite the more often he wore Western clothing and, by extension, the more frequently he sat on chairs at high tables typical of the Western style of living.'[1] A British architect was commissioned to design a building in Tokyo called the 'Rokumeikan' which functioned as a centre for social gatherings of Japanese and foreign diplomats. Here, it is claimed, Japanese ladies dressed in bustles were instructed in the principles of European cooking.

The relationship with the Western powers was double-edged, however. While, on the one hand, Japan needed allies in Great Britain, France and Germany for trade purposes, on the other it feared being seen as a kind of sub-colony. Primarily as a means of self-defence, and in an attempt to establish itself as an equal power with those industrialized countries, Japan devoted much of its newly found wealth to building up an army and a navy. A fierce sense of nationalism motivated the people in these years, on a par with that expressed in many European countries.

The programme of modernization concentrated on the establishment of new industries, and on the development of a compulsory mass education system and a modern commercial infrastructure – a banking system, railways, harbours, lighthouses, dockyards, telegraph offices, printing presses and newspapers, and post offices. Many items previously unknown in the East, such as cigars and cigarettes, were introduced into Japan. Numerous foreign experts and technicians – among them railway and marine engineers, and agricultural experts – were hired to work in Japan in the last three decades of the nineteenth century, while many young Japanese were sent abroad to Europe and the USA to study. The government took an active role in this programme of modernization, setting up model factories to encourage Japanese entrepreneurs to follow suit. In some cases, factories were established, then sold off at low prices to the large trading companies or 'zaibatsus' (which included at this time Mitsui, Mitsubishi, Sumitomo and Yasuda). These zaibatsus, which in some cases originated in prosperous merchant families in the Edo period, were to become very powerful and important.

The opportunities for entrepreneurs to set up businesses in the Meiji years and immediately afterwards were enormous. Many took advantage of them, to profit from the new technology that was suddenly available in Japan. Among the new manufacturing companies established in these years were a few fairly modest organizations which were to go on to become giants of the consumer goods industry in the years following the Second World War. What later became the Seiko group, for example,

An early radio, produced in the 1920s by the Hayakawa Electric Company, originally a metalworking concern. It changed its name to 'Sharp', today one of the leading Japanese manufacturers of electrical and electronic goods.

Two nineteenth-century Japanese prints depicting different forms of manufacture. The print on the left shows silk thread being refined; on the right work is in progress in a boot-making factory, a highly labour-intensive activity.

was originally established by Kuitaro Hattori who set up the Hattori Seiko Co. Ltd in Tokyo in 1881. This company concentrated on the production of precision machinery. Eleven years later, Hattori founded Seikosha which manufactured timepieces, although the watch division itself was not established until 1937. Similarly, the Toyoda Company formed in 1897 manufactured automatic wooden looms. Again, it was not until the 1930s that the company diversified its production, this time into motor cars, with the formation of its now famous Toyota division. Tokujio Hayakawa founded his small snap buckle and metalworks business in 1912, the final year of the Meiji period. By the 1920s it had become the Hayakawa Electric Co. Ltd, concentrating its efforts on the production of cats' whiskers radios. Much later, the company changed its name to 'Sharp' after the 'Ever-Sharp' propelling pencil that it had started to manufacture in 1915. Another leading electrical company, Matsushita, was formed in 1918, the year of Japan's post-First

World War economic boom. It began modestly with Konosuke Matsushita making adaptor sockets in his own home, but expanded in the inter-war years to become a major industrial force.

Japan is a single crop country which had depended on the production of rice for centuries. It also needed to import nearly all its raw materials and heavy machinery. To obtain these, foreign trade was vital. Exports, in the period 1868-97, increased twenty-fold, in return for the raw materials and foreign machinery needed for manufacture and modernization.

The image of its production that Japan projected in the West in the second half of the nineteenth century was not, however, one associated with modern life but rather with overtly traditional values. Westerners' perception of Japan was coloured by the richness and exoticism of, first, ukiyo-e prints, and later the densely patterned kimonos, lacquerwork, screens and fans that they imported with such fervour from the 1860s onwards. This aesthetic contrasted violently with the essential values of the ordinary Japanese people. Japanese manufacturers were quick, however, to exploit the taste for all things Oriental that developed first in Europe, and a little later in the USA. In the second half of the nineteenth century, they produced highly decorated goods especially for those markets and exported them in vast numbers to the countless warehouses that dealt in such goods.

The craze for *'Japonisme'* first took hold in Paris in the 1850s and 1860s among the avant-garde painters of the day and filtered into England through the agency of men such as James McNeill Whistler, who had worked in Paris before moving to London. Partly because the Japanese could only send small, lightweight goods on the long journey to Europe and partly because of the Victorian taste for the exotic, the European market was flooded, after 1868, with a rich array of decorative Japanese goods, among them fans, buddhas, lacquerwork, embroidery, *cloisonné* enamel, paper, sunshades and folding screens. The first major show of Japanese goods in Britain was at the 1862 exhibition where Sir Rutherford Alcock displayed his own collection of Japanese artefacts which included a range of

The 'Ever-Sharp' propelling pencil, produced in 1915 by the Hayakawa Company.

The Japanese Court at the International Exhibition held in London in 1862. The stand displayed the first examples of traditional Japanese goods to be seen in London by a large audience, and was highly influential in helping create the vogue for all things Japanese which developed in the 1870s and 1880s.

ceramics, prints, fans and textiles. The most striking features of the decoration on all the items were the stylized use of natural imagery and the strong sense of asymmetry, both of which found their way into much domestically manufactured British decorative art in the second half of the nineteenth century.

The vogue for Japanese ware had

influenced the stylistic preferences of a large section of the British middle-class market by the 1880s. A number of London stores, among them Whiteleys, Debenham and Freebody, Swan and Edgar and Liberty, opened Oriental departments to cater to the demand. Of these, Liberty was most committed to the fashion and its owner, Arthur Lasenby Liberty, visited Japan in 1888

Poster for 'The Geisha' from 1896. The influence of Japanism extended from the applied arts to popular entertainment as this event at Daly's Theatre in London clearly indicates. Probably the best-known example of this influence is Gilbert and Sullivan's operetta, 'The Mikado'.

A porcelain vase by James Hadley with moulded, painted and gilt decoration and imagery inspired by Japanese examples. The vogue for the Japanese style in the second half of the nineteenth century was particularly marked in ceramics.

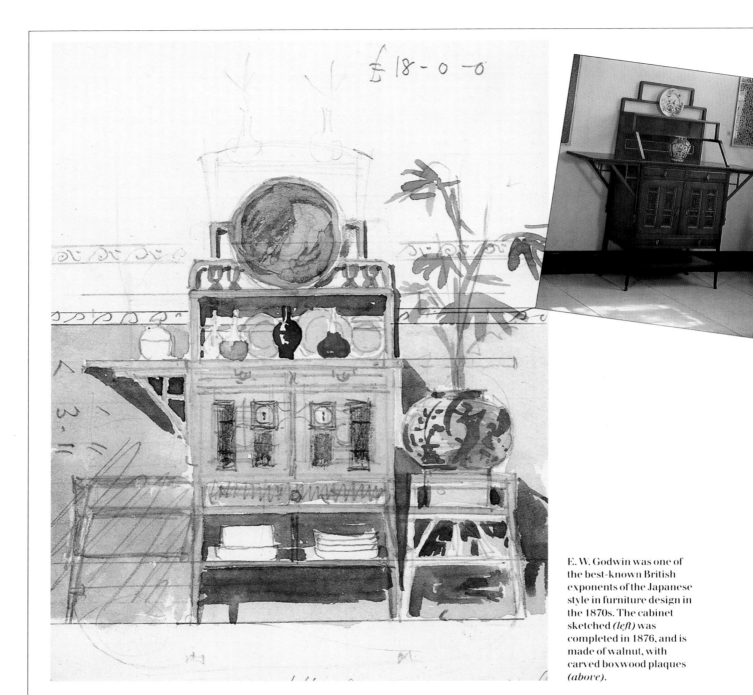

£18-0-0

E. W. Godwin was one of the best-known British exponents of the Japanese style in furniture design in the 1870s. The cabinet sketched *(left)* was completed in 1876, and is made of walnut, with carved boxwood plaques *(above)*.

in search of new goods to sell in his shop. He went on to manufacture and sell textiles produced using traditional Japanese dyeing techniques.

On a more avant-garde level '*Japonisme*' also influenced a number of architects and designers who were seeking alternatives to the British mid-nineteenth-century obsession with the Gothic Revival.

E. W. Godwin collected Japanese prints from the 1860s onwards and based many of his designs for furniture and interiors on the domestic scenes depicted in them. Thomas Jeckyll and Walter Crane similarly used prints as a source of knowledge about Japan. Only Christopher Dresser, who had visited Japan immediately after the 1868 revolution, on a commission from the British Chamber

of Commerce to report on Japanese manufacture, developed a real understanding, through firsthand experience, of the true principles of Japanese art. With them in mind, he sought to develop a more rational, functional theory of design than his contemporaries. His idea that 'utility must precede beauty'[2] derived directly from contact with the Japanese concepts of 'sabi' and 'shibui'. In 1879 Dresser opened an Oriental warehouse in Farringdon Street. A little later, in 1895, A. H. Mackmurdo executed a very simple interior along Japanese lines for Mortimer Mempes. Meanwhile, in Scotland the architect-designer C. R. Mackintosh realized his own versions of Japanese architectural structure in his houses outside Glasgow and in the Glasgow School of Art.

The impact of Japan on Europe was largely the result of its presence at large international exhibitions, including Paris 1867, Vienna 1873 – the first at which the new Meiji regime presented itself to the rest of the world – and Paris 1900. By this time, Japanese style had become one of the main sources of the French architectural and decorative art nouveau movement, particularly evident in the work of, among others, Emile Gallé and Hector Guimard. Japan provided an important stimulus to the emergence of a new, modern decoration, whether applied or structural. It did not bring about a total design revolution but it did supply a new kind of exoticism. This exoticism enabled Europe to stand back from the industrial turbulence which characterized its urban life at the turn of the century and focus on a distant unknown country producing exhilarating and refreshingly new forms of decoration with no traces of historicism.

In the USA, however, where more Japanese architecture was seen at public exhibitions, including Philadelphia's 'Centennial Exhibition' of 1876 and Chicago's 'Century of Progress' of 1893, a different set of Japanese aesthetic principles was in evidence. These had a much more dramatic influence on the progress of modern American architecture and design.

The architect who did more than any other single individual to build a modern architectural idiom on a profound understanding of traditional Japanese aesthetic principles was the American, Frank Lloyd Wright. In turn, Wright became one of the most powerful influences on the subsequent generation of architects and designers of the European Modern Movement which sprang up in Holland, Germany and France in the years following the First World War. He alone, in many ways, was responsible for mediating between

HOW SIR TRISTRAM DRANK OF THE LOVE DRINK

Among the British graphic artists inspired by the Japanese aesthetic in the nineteenth century was Aubrey Beardsley. As this illustration from his 'Tristan and Isolde' series demonstrates, he was particularly influenced by the use of line and decoration from the natural world.

Japan and the West and for establishing Japanese principles as among the most important sources of inspiration for modern architecture in the West.

Wright's first experience of Japanese architecture was at the 'Century of Progress' exhibition of 1893 where he was much taken by the Ho-o-den Pavilion. The interior of the building was full of uyiko-e prints and Wright began to collect them, travelling to Japan in 1906 to gather more. It was during this visit that he both increased his knowledge of traditional Japanese architecture and applied arts and became committed to the idea that 'Japanese art was nearer to the earth and a more indigenous product of native conditions of life and work, therefore more nearly modern, as I saw it, than any European civilization alive or dead.'[3]

This thought led him to evolve a theory of modern architecture which was founded on a number of Japanese-inspired principles. These included the central belief in the idea of the 'elimination of the insignificant'[4]; the

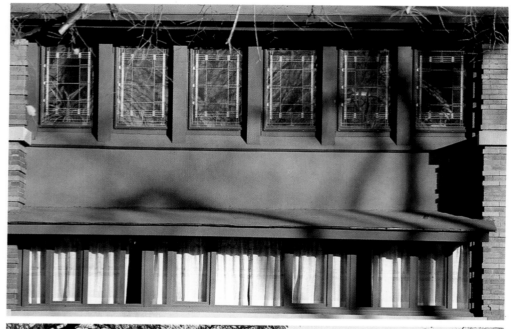

A window detail from Frank Lloyd Wright's Arthur Heurtley House of 1902 in Oak Park, Chicago. The aesthetic of the building, in particular the stress on the horizontal, is Japanese in origin.

In his Frank W. Thomas House of 1901, Frank Lloyd Wright emphasized, once again, the use of horizontal planes, thereby showing the relationship of the building to the ground on which it is built – another theme directly inspired by the model of Japan.

The continued emphasis upon horizontality and on simple geometric forms of Robie House in Chicago derives from Wright's love and understanding of traditional Japanese architecture.

importance of horizontality; the relationship between the building and its natural surroundings; the theory of modularity or standardization derived from the tatami mat; the flexibility of the building's interior space; and the importance of a ritualistic centre for the home. (Wright expressed the latter through the open fire-place in his Prairie houses.) These, and many other principles, soon became fundamental tenets of much Modern Movement architecture.

Wright's work was made available in Germany in 1910-11 through the publication of Ernst Wasmuth's two-volume study of the architect, and in Holland through the mediation of H. P. Berlage, and he became one of the major influences on the work of the next generation of Modern Movement masters. In 1914, after having built the Robie House (1908) and Taliesin (1909) – two primary examples of his interpretation of Japanese principles – Wright returned to Tokyo to start work on the Imperial Hotel which he had been commissioned to build as a base both for Western travellers in Japan and for Japanese businessmen. He resolved this difficult brief by adapting a number of essentially Japanese ideas, such as 'gravity heating' and the emphasis on horizontality, to his own ends.

In depending so strongly upon Japan as a source of inspiration, Wright developed an 'organic' rather than a 'mechanistic' metaphor as a base for his theory of architectural functionalism. It was a metaphor which was shared by many of the Modern Movement's American advocates, including the Greene brothers and, a little later, Richard Neutra. While in Europe the idea of the machine was a much more obvious source of influence, there can be little doubt that many of the Japanese-inspired architectural features that Wright developed were picked up and reused by International Style architects of the 1920s and 1930s. The 'elimination of the insignificant', the commitment to modularity, the relationship of internal with external space, and the idea that the architect should be responsible for the whole interior rather than for the architectural shell alone, became fundamental elements in Modern Movement architecture.

By the 1920s and 1930s, the International Style had moved away from overt references

Tokyo's main street after the great earthquake of 1923 shows the devastation. The loss of buildings served to encourage many new exciting architectural projects in the city.

and the Viennese Secession group.

The greatest single opportunity for Western-style architects came with the Kanto earthquake of 1923 which destroyed most of Tokyo and Yokohama and left the way open for an almost complete reconstruction of the cities. In 1926 a Japanese Secession Group emerged. A number of the new buildings, including Yamada's Central Telephone Office in Tokyo in 1926 and Tetsuro Yoshida's Tokyo General Post Office in 1931, demonstrated a clear Japanese assimilation of the International Style. The arrival of the Czech American Antonin Raymond in Japan in 1919 to work on Wright's Imperial Hotel, and his decision to stay and work there as a practising architect in the International Style, was a definite boost to the Japanese movement. Similarly, the experiences of young Japanese architects and designers who travelled to Europe either to study at the Bauhaus in Dessau or, in the cases of Junzo Sakakura and Kunio Mayekawa, to work with Le Corbusier in Paris, were of prime importance.

In 1933, the German architect Bruno Taut was invited to Japan by the Japan Architects Association. Taut had contributed an International Style building to the Weissenhof Seidlung of 1927, but was also a firm believer in using the principles of Far Eastern architecture to guide Western architects. Taut had been asked to be a consultant to the Industrial Art Institute, founded in Japan in 1928. His brief now was to advise Japan on ways of integrating the best of its traditions with its move into international Modernism. Taut stayed in Japan for three years and wrote prolifically on what he felt to be the important influence of the country's traditions upon the modern world.

Information about Western architectural theory and practice was widely available in Japan in the inter-war years. The *Nippon Architect*, for example, served as a means of disseminating ideas about the International Style in all its manifestations. In particular, in those days of extreme nationalism, it highlighted the role that Japan had played in the formulation of the International Style by publishing in 1937 Hans Eckstein's essay 'Japanese Dwelling House and Modern Architecture' and, in German, Wasmuth's 'The Japanese Living House'. In 1939, an

to Japan, but there were still signs of the relationship between East and West in architecture. In the 1930s, the emphasis on an Oriental inspiration for Modern architecture re-emerged, this time with Japan taking a much more active role in the exchange of views. A two-way communication process was initiated whereby Japanese architects and designers went to Europe to study and train, and European architects travelled to Japan to see at first hand where many of the ideas with which they were so familiar had originated.

Since the early days of the Meiji Restoration Japan had looked to Europe for much of its architectural inspiration. Soon after the Restoration a national engineering school – the National Kobu Daigakko – had been founded as a means of replacing the old apprenticeship system of carpenters and construction workers. A generation of architects emerged from that school who copied Western architecture, in particular the historicist styles of the late-nineteenth century, in their designs for banks and government buildings. Gradually, though, younger Japanese architects, among them Mamoru Yamada, began to look for ideas to more avant-garde European manifestations such as the work of Otto Wagner

Frank Lloyd Wright's Imperial Hotel in Tokyo, completed in the early 1920s. Intended both for Japanese businessmen and foreigners, stylistically the hotel was a strange hybrid of Eastern and Western architectural idioms. The hotel interior *(below)* was primarily Western in character, but included countless features which had a distinctly Japanese flavour, such as the hanging lanterns visible here.

article by the American architect Ralph T. Walker, commented on Bruno Taut's essay on Japanese architecture. Walker decried the fact that while Japanese architecture was used as an example of economy, standardization and prefabrication, no real cultural analysis accompanied what he felt was a rather superficial appropriation of Japanese architectural principles.

Another official representative of the European Modern Movement to visit Japan during this period was the French designer, Charlotte Perriand. Sakakura was the initial link between Perriand and Japan but she was invited in 1940 by the Ministry of Commerce and Industry as an adviser on industrial art. Taut's visit seven years earlier had been to advise on ways of expanding Japanese exports at a time when they were in difficulties as a result of foreign tariffs. Perriand was now asked to select a range of traditional and new products for an exhibition entitled 'Tradition, Selection, Creation' at the Takashimaya store. Clearly the aim was to let a well-trained Western eye select the best products – both old and new – in order to give Japanese manufacturers an indication of what might or might not export well to Europe. Like Taut, Perriand was fascinated by Japan and stayed there for three years. In 1942 she wrote a book entitled *Contact with Japan* and in 1943 left for Indo-China on her way back to France.

The first indication that Japan was succeeding in finding a satisfactory path between East and West in its search for its own version of the International Style came at the Paris Exhibition of 1937 where Sakakura designed the Japanese pavilion. It served mainly as a vehicle for nationalistic propaganda, showing the West the level and range of contemporary Japanese manufacturing capability. The pavilion itself was an essentially Modern building – both in its construction and its appearance – consisting of two floors and including a suspended ramp. Many of its features derived, however, from traditional Japanese architecture, among them its open plan, the use of natural materials, the relationship between the building and the garden and the inclusion of a tea-room. The intention was clearly to show just how much the Corbusian brand of Modernist architecture depended upon fundamental Japanese principles. Inside the building a link between the old and the new was sustained by the inclusion of a range of traditional household goods – ceramics, carpets, and furniture – and examples of decorative art, including objects in porcelain, lacquer and fabric. These were exhibited alongside blown-up photographs and films of Japanese manufacturing techniques and a range of products from the new industries, including heating devices, an electric record player and an electric clock, all manufactured by the Matsushita Company.

Japan's drive to sustain its export trade in the depressed years of the 1930s was, however, a somewhat futile exercise. In 1936 the Japanese Association of Design and Industries was formed as part of this effort but the world economic and political situation was by then such that hopes for a return to the healthy period which followed the First World War were ill-founded. After the advances made in the 'golden years' (1900-18), the 1920s and 1930s were dominated by economic depression. Although the Japanese automobile industry was born in the 1930s its only clients, at that time, were the government and the army. The only area of design to thrive in the recession was advertising, which flourished through the 1930s as a means of trying to entice the people to spend their money on consumer durables. Industrial design, usually a survivor in a recession, was not established firmly enough in Japan to be able to come into its own. Modernist architecture, as we have seen, had a moment of glory in the late 1920s and early 1930s but it was not really until the years after the Second World War that a truly modern Japanese architecture finally emerged to compete successfully on the international scene.

Junzo Sakakura's Pavilion, built for the international exhibition held in Paris in 1937, represented the first moment when a Japanese architect, trained in the West, set out to fuse Western Modernism with traditional Japanese architectural themes.

Advertising was the one area of design to flourish in Japan in the 1930s. These posters for the Shiseido cosmetics company date from 1938 and 1939 (right).

Handicrafts were threatened with extinction by the onslaught of mass production and only survived through the promotional efforts of a few reforming individuals and critics, among them Soetsu Yanagi and Kunio Yanagida.

The 1930s are described in Japan as the decade of the 'dark valley'. They were characterized by a rising surge of ultra-nationalism and militarism culminating, first, in the war with China in 1937 and then, four years later, the Pacific War. Socially, a huge gulf divided the rich from the poor in these years and there was a great deal of unrest among the ranks of the newly formed urban proletariat. Modernization and Westernization had taken place on a massive scale in the decades since the 1860s but by the inter-war years this had resulted as much in confusion as anything else.

In the years 1860-1940 Japan gave more to the West than it received in return, particularly in the areas of art, architecture and design. None the less, the technological advances made in Japan in these years, which depended almost entirely on imports from the West, were substantial. After the Second World War, in spite of the massive destruction, Japan was in a position to gather its strengths very quickly and to take up where it had left off. By then also it was ready to assimilate many of the aesthetic lessons it had both taught, and learned from, the West and to move into a new epoch. In the post-war years, the Japanese provided, once again in the areas of architecture, crafts and graphic design, and for the first time in fashion, electrical and electronic goods, and automotive design, a model for the rest of the world.

Chapter 2

From Pre-Modern to Modern: Japanese industry, society and design after 1945

'Where once the Americans paternally fostered Japan's post-war reconstruction, they now stand aghast at the competitor which has emerged'[1]

The dramatic changes that occurred in Japan in the years immediately following the bombing of Hiroshima and Nagasaki were reminiscent of the revolution of the 1860s. Within a decade a transformation had taken place, on economic, social, technological and cultural fronts simultaneously, which changed Japan from a war-weary country with nothing to one of the most powerful manufacturing forces in the world. In 1945, as B. Entwhistle explains, 'the stores were pathetically short of consumer goods and it was obvious that most people were making do with old clothes. Almost the only automobiles on the streets were US army cars, since no gasoline was available for civilian use'.[2] Less than a decade later, however, industrial production had reached the level of twenty years earlier and, in terms of their purchasing power, personal incomes had been restored to their pre-war level. Between 1960 and 1978 Japan's national income grew at over 8 per cent per year and even in 1980, when the boom had waned, Japan's manufacturing output still managed to rise by 6 per cent.

The reasons for this dramatic resurgence were, inevitably, complex. Primary among them were the availability of American funding, supplied as part of the USA's continuing fight against Communism (in 1947, for example, American aid to Japan amounted to 400 million dollars); the outbreak of the Korean War in 1951 which necessitated the manufacture of supplies for the fighting services; and the awareness on the part of the Japanese government, from

the mid-1940s onwards, of the need to develop a strong export market based on a sound domestic market.

The presence of American troops in Japan between 1945 and 1952, under the leadership of General MacArthur, had an enormous impact, culturally as well as economically. It introduced Western ideas of

democracy and freedom, and provided a means for the Japanese to gain access to the advanced technological knowledge and skills of the USA. Another significant influence was America's refusal to allow vast sums of money to be used in the development of a Japanese armed service. This benefited the manufacturing sector

A view of the city of Hiroshima in March 1946 showing the complete devastation effected by the American bombing of the previous year.

General MacArthur, accompanied by Lieutenant-General Sutherland and President Sergio Osmena of the Philippine Republic.

War-time bombing destroyed nearly all the buildings in Tokyo; the emphatically high-rise architecture of the contemporary city dates from post-1945.

A motorcycle assembly plant in Japan. Along with optical and precision instruments and electronic equipment, motorcycles were one of the high-technology products which characterized Japan's post-war industrial reconstruction.

which had access to greater funds than might otherwise have been available.

The early years of the occupation were characterized by a strict programme of reform and retribution, manifested in the purging of key individuals associated with the pre-war and wartime regimes and the dissolution of the zaibatsus (the trading houses). By 1948, however, the zaibatsus were re-emerging – albeit on a more modest scale than before – and many of the pre-war business leaders were reinstated in positions of power. Japan was also allowed to resume trade with foreign countries. By the following year Japan had moved towards a position of social and economic stability, and by 1950 was ready to surge forward. In 1951 the Japanese peace treaty was signed and in the following year independence granted. From that moment onwards, in spite of minor economic setbacks in 1953 and 1958, the country was geared to increased production levels and enhanced prosperity. The 'economic miracle' was underway, reaching a peak in the second half of the 1960s and lasting into the early 1970s.

Many explanations have been put forward for the phenomenal growth pattern of Japanese manufacturing in the years following 1950, some of them culturally, and others economically, based. One of the cultural factors usually advanced is the concept which economist Keith Smith has described as 'mutual commitment',[3] that is, the loyalty that each Japanese citizen feels for the group, over and above his or her personal interest. Inside manufacturing industry this has been manifested in such ideas as the 'life-time contract' (a phenomenon which is, however, becoming less common in Japan in the 1980s); the protective paternalism of the employer towards his employees; and the enhanced sense of loyalty of the employee for the company, expressed by the singing of company songs, the wearing of company uniforms and the widespread use of company slogans.

The industrial harmony that has, for the most part, resulted from this special relationship between management and workforce without doubt facilitated the emergence of Japan's manufacturing strength after the war. That strength does not, however, simply result from these deeply rooted cultural forces. Ideas imported from abroad and deliberate policy decisions on the part of management and of the Japanese government are just as significant. The most notable importation in management terms was that of the 'quality control circle', a concept borrowed from American business practice. It received a special welcome on Japanese soil and (along with bonus incentives) has remained one of the most influential factors in motivating the loyalty of the workforce. Nearly all the large manufacturing companies encourage their employees to participate in the quality control of the goods it produces and to organize 'work circles' which allow factory workers to make suggestions about production improvement. These initiatives help to keep manufacturing standards high

and provide a sense of involvement for each and every employee.

There are other factors that contributed to Japan's post-war economic achievement. The most important are the close co-operation of the zaibatsus – Mitsui, Mitsubishi, and others – with the state, and the special nature of Japan's so-called 'dual economy'. This favours the emergence of large-scale corporations alongside the retention of small, workshop-based concerns, which act as sub-contractors to the major companies to supply them with components. Nobutaka Ike has written that 'in 1969 roughly one-half of all establishments engaged in manufacturing and almost eighty per cent of those engaged in the wholesale and retail trade, employed only from one to four persons. In the back

alleys of Tokyo are numerous small shops where workmen make parts for bicycles, vacuum cleaners and other appliances'.[4] This 'dual' system allowed the large-scale companies a degree of flexibility unknown in countries like the USA where the 'big is beautiful' principle has dominated many aspects of production. Economists have also discussed at great length the concept of 'flexible specialization' as partly responsible for Japan's achievements. This is the idea that within mass production there is, at all times, room for product innovation and variation. Where design is concerned it is clearly an important concept, as without it Ford's idea of product standardization is inevitable and design innovation is minimized. Flexibility in Japanese manufacture is enhanced by an emphasis on

The Japanese automobile industry became increasingly important after the Second World War although the styling of the products reflected American and European models for some time. The Toyota RS (Crown) of 1955 is typical of the American orientation in Japanese automobiles in this period.

electronically controlled manufacturing systems which make immediate re-programming possible, and thereby facilitate change.

A final factor in the story of Japan's reconstruction is the role of the government's highly defined industrial policy and the special role played by MITI (the Ministry of International Trade and Industry) in the years following the Second World War. The need to export goods became an economic imperative and there was a widely held belief that if manufacturers produced goods of adequate quality, competitively priced, they would inevitably find a place in world markets. This was founded on the fact, according to Ike, that 'the destruction caused by war, combined with the slowdown in maintenance of all kinds of equipment and facilities, produced a pent-up demand for goods and services throughout the world.'[5]

Established in 1949, MITI helped Japanese manufacturers in several ways – by investing in and subsidizing companies, making trade agreements, sponsoring legislation and offering advice. As such, it played a central part in the post-war export drive, encouraging the specialized production of those goods which had a cost advantage for Japan, controlling the import and use of foreign technology, assisting research and development, and helping getting new firms

Sony's Type 'G' tape-recorder of 1950, a bulky object which owed much to war-time technological discoveries, was the first of its kind in Japan and represented a coup for the company.

established. For example, MITI granted the Sony Corporation (established in 1946 as Tokyo Tsushin Kabushiki Kaisha and renamed in 1957) permission to spend part of Japan's limited foreign exchange on acquiring from the American firm Western Electric the manufacturing rights to the recently invented transistor. As a result, Sony produced its first transistor radio in 1955. This kind of assistance was typical. While some projects, such as the attempt to consolidate the car industry around Nissan and Toyota, were failures, MITI's rebuilding of the Japanese textile industry was an irrefutable success. The development of synthetic fibres in Japan was due almost entirely to MITI's efforts to import technology from abroad and to encourage research and development in that area.

The new industries of the late 1950s concentrated on technically advanced and capital intensive goods such as motorcycles, cameras and audio equipment (in addition to ships and petrochemicals). All these were helped by MITI, which later also put its efforts into video equipment and domestic appliances. It even extended its interests into the area of design itself, creating, in 1957, a body called the Industrial Design Promotion Council. Set up initially to deal with foreign claims against the illegal use of copying by Japanese enterprises, it became highly influential in the boom years of the 1960s.

The success of Japanese exports was also dependent upon the health of the home market, and the story of the transformation of Japanese society after 1945 is a necessary parallel to that of the country's industrial expansion. Ike wrote that 'During the first few years of the occupation, Japan was probably subjected to more Western influence than during the several decades which preceded it'.[6] This process of Westernization characterized the decades following the war. A dramatic social revolution took place: people flooded from the rural areas to the reconstructed cities in the 1950s and 1960s in search of work, and Japan became a predominantly urban country. The products of the new industries – among them television sets, refrigerators and washing machines – which in 1950 had been almost unknown in Japanese homes, were ubiquitous by the end of the decade and the electrical and electronic 'gadget' became

The Datsun SP 212 sports car *(top)* was put into production by the Nissan Company in 1960. Its twin tones and sleek body-curves derived from American examples.

Sharp's all-transistor electronic, desk-top calculator of 1964 was the first example of its kind in the world. Its bulky forms were transformed by the 1970s move towards miniaturization.

a commonplace, crowding the surfaces of previously highly austere interiors. Toshiba, for instance, produced the first electric rice-cooker in 1955 and this object quickly became a necessity for the young couple setting up home. Soon the home market was well supplied with electrical gadgets which rapidly came to be seen as essentials rather than luxuries by the new, affluent, consumers. A consumer society developed through the 1960s with the result that individual comfort and 'life-style' became more important than the interests of the group. A growing individualism characterized the changing social patterns of these years and by the end of the 1960s the traditional Japanese society of the 1940s had all but disappeared.

The changing role of women in this period was also of prime importance in the developing patterns of consumption within Japanese society. Women took on a more assertive role within the household, as well as becoming a greater part of the work-force, with the result that they made more and more purchasing decisions, particularly where goods for the home were concerned. Women became an important target market for the manufacturers. Twinned with this was the dramatic rise of an affluent youth market – a result of high employment and generous starting salaries. Japanese couples tended to marry and set up home early, and with high wages they could afford to indulge in a wide range of consumer goods. Even unmarried teenagers became avid consumers, buying goods from audio equipment to cameras and watches. The inordinately high price of housing in Japan meant that few people could afford to buy their own homes and so they tended to spend most of their expendable incomes on goods rather than housing.

The readiness of both the domestic and the export markets to buy Japanese consumer goods in the decades following the Second World War meant that, at first, there was little need to attend to more than availability, adequate quality, efficient technology and price. Gradually, as more manufacturers came on to the market, competition increased, and the seller's market gave way, increasingly, to a buyer's market. It became apparent that the goods needed to compete on more than mere price and that product

An early microwave oven, or 'electronic range' as it was then called, pioneered by the Sharp Company in 1962. Crudely designed and constructed, this was among the first of many more sophisticated models later manufactured by the same company.

By 1960, Sharp had moved into the mass-production of colour television sets on a large scale. This model from that year shows a debt to American automotive styling in the chrome details on its control panel.

appearance and quality were also becoming increasingly important. Although, in the area of high-technology goods, this awareness took a while to develop, many efforts were initiated in the 1950s to ensure that 'design' would become part of Japan's manufacturing formula.

The first stirrings of an awareness of the need to ally design with the industrial renaissance of the post-war years were felt in the early 1950s, and its first manifestations were educational in nature. Two conflicting theories about design, in relation to industry, were imported into Japan in these years – one from America and the other from Europe. The less common highly commercial American model favoured the consultant industrial designer. The other, a more 'purist' non-commercial architecture-dominated European example, came to Japan through the Bauhaus's pedagogical philosophy.

The chief protagonist of Bauhaus thinking was the critic Masaru Katsumie who worked on the periodical *Industrial Art News* from 1948 to 1949 and went on to become a major promoter of the European-inspired notion of 'good design' in Japan. Not only did he revive the ideas behind the 1920s debate at the Bauhaus between Johannes Itten's intuitive approach to design and Laszlo Moholy-Nagy's rationalist stance, he also introduced many foreign books about design, among them Herbert Read's *Art and Industry*, into Japan. Katsumie has named 1950 'the first year of design' in Japan and it was between then and 1955 that many of Japan's leading design educational institutions were formed. These were the Creative Art Education Institute (1951), the Kuwazawa Design School (1954), and the Visual Art Education Centre (1955). While Katsumie was instrumental in the formation of many of these institutions, he was solely responsible, in 1954, for the creation of the Society for the Science of Design which sought to study design from a rational, systematic perspective

in the European, Constructivist tradition.

In 1953 the presence of a growing design lobby in Japan was recognized internationally by the request for Japan to participate in the tenth Milan Triennale to be held in the following year. Isamu Kenmochi, one of the best-known names in Japanese industrial design at this time, and the head of the design department at the Industrial Arts Institute, replied that he felt that Japan was not ready to exhibit in an international design arena. It was decided, instead, that the links between media and design fields should be strengthened so that Japan could take part in the eleventh Triennale in 1957.

There were two other major design promotion initiatives in the 1950s. The first

was the formation in 1952 of JIDA (the Japanese Industrial Designers' Association). This was followed in 1957 by the instigation by the Industrial Design Promotion Council of a system of awarding prizes (the 'G' mark) to what were considered to be well-designed goods. Katsumie was critical of the value of government intervention in this area and felt, instead, that a subcommittee of design experts should be formed to develop a more comprehensive design policy. In 1959 such a subcommittee was created with the brief to formulate 'An Advanced Policy of Design for Japan'. In 1973 Katsumie wrote that he felt that 'by its very nature the design movement belongs . . . outside the government's domain. The task devolves primarily upon

This simple television set, manufactured by Sharp in 1953, coincided with the first Japanese television broadcasts.

independent interested designers, with the possible support of the intelligent public. From the outset I placed my hopes on a movement arising spontaneously among designers and extending to the public.'[7]

The proliferation of further design organizations in the 1950s certainly fuelled his hopes, partly because they crossed a number of design disciplines. These organizations included the Japan Advertising Artists' Club (1951), the Tokyo Art Directors' Club (1952), the Japan Design Committee (1953), the Japan Designer-Craftsman Association (1956), and the Japan Interior Designers' Association (1958).

All these societies were concerned with the need for professionalism in design and recognition of the designer's status. They wanted either to upgrade the image of designers or promote their activities. Their function as designers' unions tended to vary however. JIDA, for one, developed a strong union orientation which, according to Katsumie, was the reason for three leading Japanese designers of the 1950s – Isamu Kenmochi, Sori Yanagi and Watanabe Riki – withdrawing their membership.

The Japan Design Committee, which included members from a wide spectrum of design activities – among them architecture, interior design, industrial and graphic design and crafts – was founded on the occasion of Japan's being asked to participate at the Milan Triennale. It went on to organize the World Design Conference of 1960, the first international design event to be held in Tokyo. This was an important event in that the generation of designers that participated was to dominate the profession through the 1960s. Among them was Kenji Ekuan who became a prominent consultant designer through the 1960s and 1970s, and the first such Japanese designer to gain international recognition.

In spite of Katsumie's misgivings about the government's role in the promotion of Japanese design activities of the 1950s, there can be no doubt that its initiatives were a very important aspect in propaganda terms of Japan's bid for a national identity in world markets. The promotion of design paralleled very closely the expansion of manufacturing industry. Design was seen as a key element in the production, marketing and consumption of Japanese high-technology goods both at

The 'G' mark, awarded to well-designed goods, was initiated in 1957. The XA Olympus camera, designed by the consultant design group GK Associates, was awarded the 'G' mark in 1982. It remains one of the most respected of recent camera designs to emerge from Japan. Honda's three-door version of its compact Civic *(top)* was awarded the 'G' mark in 1984.

Sony developed the world's
first solid state television
receiver, featuring an
eight-inch screen and
weighing only thirteen
pounds, in 1959.

home and abroad. Awareness of design has
become an intrinsic element in Japan's bid
for international cultural recognition.

While design promotion was pursued
energetically through the 1950s and 1960s by
the government and by a small group of
interested individuals associated with design
education and criticism, the number of
achievements in design were minimal at
first. Japanese manufacturers found it
difficult to rid their goods of the image of
being cheap and inferior. On the whole the
goods still carried with them their pre- and
early post-war reputation for being, in the
words of Keith Smith, 'cheap, imitative and
shoddy', better known for their technical
reliability and their competitive prices than
for their design.

One of the reasons for this was that many
companies did not employ designers at all.
'Design' was a function of the engineering
and production departments. The most
familiar image of Japanese goods abroad
was the one associated with the
'technological look'. This aesthetic was
common to motorcycles, cameras and audio
equipment and, when it did not simply
emulate American examples, it reflected a
somewhat crude manipulation of the
technological components involved. There
were exceptions, of course, and by the 1950s
a handful of companies were conscious of
the need for an in-house design team to
create identities for their products. Honda,
for instance, had its own design team by
1957, and in 1958 Japan's National Railways
established a design committee.

Probably the most progressive company in
this respect was Sony. Although in its early
days in the late 1940s, the corporation's
engineers were responsible for both its
products' interiors and exteriors, as early as
1951 Sony sought the advice of designers
who were still trained as illustrators and
painters, rather than as designers for
industry. Sori Yanagi, who became one of
Japan's best-known industrial designers
internationally, was commissioned to design
the 'H' tape-recorder which was marketed in
1952-3. In 1954, Sony hired its first full-time
in-house designer and by 1961 it had 17
designers on its staff under the design
management of Norio Ohga (in the mid-
1980s he became president of the Sony
Corporation). It was some time before they

were grouped as a team and centralized, and until 1977 there were still designers scattered among different departments. By 1981, Sony had 56 designers in total, and by 1983 this had expanded to 131, located centrally in its Product Planning Centre in Tokyo under the leadership of Yasuo Kuroki. This relocation of the designers reflected their changing role from stylists to product innovators, from their performing a fairly superficial task to their becoming increasingly integrated in the processes of manufacturing and marketing.

By the early 1980s the importance of design had become much more widely recognized, whether because of the example of Sony or the effects of government efforts. Many leading Japanese high-technology manufacturing companies had large design teams, usually located within the marketing departments but with direct links with the production engineers.

The Japanese approach to industrial design, by which the majority of high-technology goods were produced, favours in-house anonymous individuals, or teams,

who received no personal credit or international recognition for their work. Where corporate design was concerned, the company name was much more important than the name of the individual designer. The role of the consultant designer was very restricted. Only Kenji Ekuan and a few others succeeded in stepping outside this system. In the late 1950s, objects such as the Japan Sewing Machine Company's domestic sewing machine, designed by M. Katsuyama and K. Hamada, demonstrated that Japan could deal with sophisticated product form

Japan's famous 'Bullet train', the Shinkansen, was introduced in 1964. In appearance, it had much in common with earlier American streamlined locomotives.

Isamu Matsunaga's
'Ancient Fantasy' textile
design of 1986. A number of
Japanese artist-craftsmen
of the 1980s combine
traditional Japanese craft
techniques with
contemporary imagery.

with a minimal approach reminiscent of that preferred by Germany. Goods like these reflected a switch from the USA to Europe as a target market.

Another instance of the use of a consultant designer in Japan was in the manufacture of furniture required by the occupational armies. The first recorded contract between a Japanese manufacturer and a consultant designer was that between the Toyo Kogyo Company and the designer Jiro Kosugi who designed the front cover (hood) of a small

tricycle (three-wheeled) truck for them. Other early examples include the Nissan Motor Company asking Shozo Sato to design a car, the result of which was the Datsun.

One reason why Japanese designers were relatively slow to come to grips with high-technology products, in contrast to their long-standing abilities in the areas of architecture, graphic design, dress design and craft, was their dependence on imported production technology, and the consequent difficulty of finding what could be called a

'Japanese style'. The problem of translating Japanese aesthetic concepts into new, non-traditional goods, manufactured with foreign tools, was enormous and one which Japanese industrial designers confronted head on in the early post-war years. The hybrid nature of the products made it impossible for designers to refer to their own aesthetic traditions – the grid concept derived from traditional architecture was utterly inappropriate in the design of a car which was all curves, for instance – and it was some time before designers were sufficiently well acquainted with the new products to tackle their design adequately.

In 1960, the year of the Tokyo World Design Conference, the Japan Design House was established in Tokyo; this was followed, in 1961, by the foundation of the Osaka Design House. Although the goods selected to be shown in these institutions were drawn from both a wide range of traditional crafts – objects in bamboo, wicker, rattan, lacquer, wood and ceramic, for example – and new electrical appliances and vehicles, the difference between these two categories was all too apparent.

The concept of design in post-war Japan was never static. From its early days as the stylistic imitation of foreign examples, design had, by the 1970s and 1980s, evolved in such a way as to become a much more integrated process within technological research and manufacture and an increasingly essential element within marketing. With the development of the concepts of 'flexible specialization' and 'cultural variation' that superseded Japan's earlier manufacturing policy of standardized mass production, design took an increasingly significant profile within the success or otherwise of Japan's trading programme. This was particularly apparent after the mid-1970s when the international oil crisis caused Japan's boom of the 1950s and 1960s to level off. Also, as the structure of Japanese society became less homogeneous and more hierarchical in the 1980s and the idea of 'life-style' became all-pervasive, design was re-defined accordingly.

Many companies, which until the mid-1970s had depended either on imported foreign models of design or on a commercial formula which ignored the concept altogether, were now forced to define their design policies quite specifically. The Toyota Company, for instance, which by the early 1980s had a design department of 430, defined design as 'the means of harmonizing human needs and mechanical requirements'. While their products were essentially conservative and sold much more on the basis of 'value for money' than on stylistic innovation, the process of design – from sketching to prototyping – was an essential component of their manufacturing structure and depended on the work of the

specialist, highly trained designer. An advanced design group also existed to show, if only in renderings and models, that the company was at least aware of the need for product innovation even if these ideas were slow to filter down into production models.

Sharp's design dictum in the early 1980s was 'priority on easy operation', which meant that the 200-strong design staff employed by the company's Corporate Design Centre existed, essentially, to make sure the products worked, and to provide

direct links with demand. In the area of high-technology goods it was particularly important that the products both looked usable to the uneducated public and *were* usable by them. Other functions of Sharp's design team included envisaging 'future living', that is, projecting and predicting the life-styles of the future, and creating consumer demand.

By the 1980s, the structure of the Product Planning Centre at Sony was the most sophisticated of all the corporate design

Sharp was at the forefront in the evolution of the hand-held electronic calculator. This model, which incorporates a liquid crystal display, was produced in 1973.

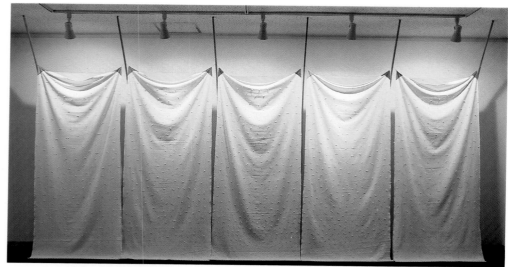

Jun Mitsuhashi's 'Soft Wall' of 1985 *(top)* demonstrates the extent to which Japanese craft, in this case textiles, retains its links with traditional aesthetics. Nissan's Pulsar 1600 (the 1986 'G'-mark model is shown above), on the other hand, represents the importance of advanced technology and mass production in contemporary Japanese design.

set-ups. It provided a co-ordinating function for the marketing, engineering, advertising, sales and promotion departments and covered a wide spectrum of activities from corporate and display design, to creating advanced products, and working on production models. Uniquely at Sony, the design department initiated a number of projects, subsequently sending them on to the research and development team rather than, as was usual practice, simply developing what that team passed on to them. Another of Sony's special contributions lay in the fact that it was not using design as a means of 'adding value' to existing technology but as a fundamental element of technically innovative products. This was in sharp contrast to those European companies such as Bang and Olufsen and Olivetti, with which it saw itself in direct competition.

In the 1980s Japan's high-technology companies have devoted a very high proportion of their annual turnover to research and development. Sony allocated 10 per cent in 1983, Canon between 7 and 8 per cent. Canon also employed an extensive design team of 65, which broke down into task forces of seven when a new project was initiated. The company defined its design philosophy with the slogan 'products with few defects', identifying design alongside quality and efficiency. At Ricoh, another company which like Canon had by the early 1980s moved from cameras into the expanding area of office machinery, the slogan was 'technology with a human touch'. The company, which had a design team of 34, believed firmly in the concept of sensitivity towards cultural variations and provided different colour codings in its products for different countries, on, for example, the control panel of its photocopier. Sony also employed this concept in its television sets, providing wood-veneer cases for Britain, metal cases for Germany and plastic cases for Italy. Inevitably, this task lay at the feet of the designer.

The status of Japanese design in the area of high-technology goods after 1945 is, finally, inseparable from the country's programme of industrial expansion and its particular industrial policies and strategies. While individuals and institutions promoting design in the 1950s had adopted a highly idealistic European-based theory, the

One of the most marked Japanese advances of the 1980s was in fashion where a few key individuals achieved international renown. Among them was Yohji Yamamoto, whose comfortable, casual clothing was a worldwide success.

manufacturers themselves were much more pragmatic, defining the design process and the role of the designer in ways that conformed to their overall corporate philosophies. Design became a very fragmented and intangible activity in industry, the product of a team rather than of a single individual's vision. The question of 'product style' also became, as a result, part of a much larger question about the role of Japanese goods in the world economy.

In those design areas – architecture, graphics, fashion and craft – which fell outside the programme of industrial expansion and which had more obvious links with Japanese culture prior to industrialization, a more direct relationship existed between the importation of design ideas from abroad, Japanese traditional aesthetics and what could be called a Japanese post-war design movement. Architecture, craft and graphic design had firm roots in the pre-war period and drew directly on Japanese traditions, and upon Western models imported from the turn of the century onwards. The links with traditional practices in these areas meant that it was much simpler to find ways of integrating the past with the present to create an exciting new hybrid. Even in the area of fashion, albeit a new, Western-influenced area of activity in Japan which took a hold in the 1970s, links with traditional artefacts and manufacturing techniques were maintained. The emphasis on simple and uncluttered styles, and the use of natural fabrics and dyes facilitated a fairly straightforward transition into the international arena. By the beginning of the 1980s, Japanese architects, craftsmen, graphic and fashion designers had made a huge impact both at home and abroad and had added these areas of expertise to Japan's long-held reputation for aesthetic quality. Gradually the areas of electronic goods and transport were added to the list and it was clear that Japan had become the home not only of modern technology but also of modern design.

PART TWO
Chapter 3

Electrical and
electronic goods

In recent years Japanese advanced technology has become synonymous with excellence. After the Second World War the Japanese committed themselves fully to a programme of technological experimentation and development as an essential part of their redevelopment. Its results were soon apparent in all areas of industrial output, especially in those new consumer goods which actually owed their existence to modern technology. Vast numbers of electrical and electronic products rolled off Japanese assembly lines in the first post-war decade.

However, at this early stage of their evolution, most of these goods displayed more sophistication in their technology than in their appearance, which was, for the most part, more a result of technical and economic demands than of aesthetic choice. It is only in fairly recent years that the concept of 'design' as we know it in the West has fully penetrated this area of Japanese production. Before, production and marketing were determined by selling the concept of 'advanced technology', and it has been a gradual process over 30 years for design to assert itself.

The huge technological advances of the immediate post-war years and the rapid emergence of a domestic market in Japan provided great opportunities for the electrical industry, which it was quick to grasp. In this, it was aided by its enlightened attitude to industrial teamwork (see chapter 2). America too made considerable contributions to the Japanese boom by offering economic subsidy, industrial relations philosophy, and scientific progress. The latter, in particular, was quickly exploited by the Japanese: for instance, on returning from a visit to General Electric in the early 1950s with an early silicon chip, Taizo Ishigaki, the chairman of Hitachi, had exclaimed that 'this little thing is going to revolutionize our company and all of Japanese business'.[1] Although it was some time before this piece of foresight was realized, by the end of the decade Japan had already understood and exploited the commercial implications of the 'electronic revolution' and its electronic consumer goods were, along with those manufactured in the USA, among the most sophisticated in the world.

The Japanese urge for technological innovation was not entirely a development of the post-1945 period. In the early decades of the century, a number of forward-thinking manufacturers moved into the production of goods with a high technological profile. In the specific area of electrical manufacturing the Sharp Company, for example, was founded in 1912 as a small metal-working business producing snap buckles, but, by the mid-1920s it had expanded into the mass production of crystal radio sets. Equally the Matsushita Electrical Company, established in 1918, and later better known by its brand name 'National', continued, after 1945, to expand on the basis of its earlier achievements in electrical engineering.

While a few companies like these had emerged in the years immediately before and after the First World War, there was a hiatus in the succession of new electrical companies until after the Second World War when many of today's best-known electrical and electronics manufacturers were born, capitalizing on wartime technological developments. The Sony Corporation, for instance, was established in May 1945 by Masaru Ibuka and Akio Morito on the basis of breakthroughs made in telecommunications engineering during the war. The corporation rapidly applied its energies to peacetime developments and the Japanese export drive.

The post-war manufacturers of consumer products tended to concentrate at first on precision optical and acoustic instruments – namely watches, cameras, tape-recorders, transistor radios, record players and amplifiers. There were several reasons for this: these objects were small enough to export in large numbers – a basic requirement of Japanese production at this time – they were goods for which there was an ever-expanding world market, and they benefited directly from the new technology. When

Sharp console video television While on the whole Japanese designers of smaller pieces of electronic audio and video equipment have moved away from the 'furniture' image, it has been retained in some larger items, like this video television, through the use of the wood-effect laminate finish.

Brother Electra 25 JP16-2SL typewriter 1984 The sophisticated wedge shape of this electronic typewriter is heavily influenced by the work of Mario Bellini for Olivetti, the Italian typewriter manufacturing company.

public television broadcasts began in Japan in the early 1950s manufacturers were quick to diversify into television sets, and through the 1950s and 1960s, as markets emerged, they produced more and more domestic appliances. By the early 1960s office equipment, in particular desk-top calculators, had been added to the list of objects which benefited from developments in electronic technology, and which Japanese companies, such as Sharp, developed for the home and export markets.

The domestic market for consumer goods grew quickly after the war. There are numerous reasons for this expansion (see chapter 2), but as far as electrical 'labour-saving' goods were concerned the disappearance of a servant class was an important factor. As one chronicler of

Japanese life explained in 1984, 'Thirty years or so ago, every middle-class Japanese family enjoyed the services of at least one live-in maid, but today, because of high wages and the exorbitant cost of a house or apartment big enough to include a maid's room, only extremely well-to-do Japanese can afford servants.'[2]

This change in living conditions led, inevitably, to an increase in the popularity of labour-saving devices and, by the mid-1980s, it had become commonplace for Japanese homes, small as they are, to be stuffed full of every conceivable kind of household gadget, in addition to a wide range of leisure equipment. (The same chronicler noted what he described as 'a national addiction to gadgetry'.[3]) A huge jump in television ownership occurred in 1964 when the Olympic Games were held in Tokyo and increased to the extent that twenty years later it had become usual for a household to own two or three sets. Consumption of domestic technological goods continued to rise dramatically in the 30 years after 1955, making it increasingly easy for

manufacturers to find outlets for their ever-widening ranges of consumer products. There was an emphasis upon a new growing market of young, affluent, highly fashion-conscious married couples who aspired not only to the more established goods – among them electric refrigerators, washing machines, vacuum cleaners and automatic rice cookers – but also, as time went on, expected to be able to buy new products such as air-conditioners and electronic ovens. The conspicuous consumption of such goods became, increasingly, a mark of social status.

Domestic consumption was not, however, the only question to preoccupy manufacturers of electrical goods in the years following the Second World War. A country of few natural resources, Japan has had to import raw materials for many years and it has continually needed secondary goods to export in exchange for them. 'Export or die' had been a battle-cry since the 1920s, but by the 1950s it had become an even more urgent requirement and considerable effort was devoted to the export trade.

Sharp microwave oven 1980s Due to its compactness, the microwave oven proved an ideal product for many Japanese manufacturers of electronic goods. The complex graphic details on this model by Sharp are typical of Japanese goods produced with the 'high-tech' look.

Sony TR55 transistor radio Sony was the first company in Japan to produce a transistor radio. The TR55, the appearance of which owed much to contemporary American styling, was the company's first export.

Cameras, watches, and other electronic and electrical goods were high on the list of potential exports and before long Toshiba, Hitachi, Hayakawa, Matsushita, Mitsubishi, Sony, Sansui, Seiko, Canon, Asahi, Pentax, Nikon, Olympus, Minolta, Ricoh, and others had found niches for their products in both the American and European market-places. This was achieved by determined programmes of aggressive marketing.

The attitude of the manufacturers towards the design of their products, whether for home or for foreign consumption, has changed dramatically with the products' growing success. Since the start of industrialization, Japan has pursued a policy of imitation or 'leap-frogging' where design is concerned, emulating the appearance of foreign models and then trying to improve upon them technically. The Hayakawa Electrical Company is typical in this respect. Its products of the inter-war years were, in essence, copies of American and European ones: its radios were enclosed in wooden cabinets with fretwork on their fronts in Gothic or art deco styles, and one wooden model of 1938 very closely resembled Wells Coates' famous round bakelite radio designed for the English E. K. Cole Company. Only one

model manufactured by Hayakawa reflected indigenous artistic traditions. It was set in a cabinet the surface of which was embellished by a painting in traditional Japanese lacquer, but this item was made as a 'special' gift, rather than as a commercial venture. After the war the company went on to manufacture console television sets in wood-veneered cabinets, following a particularly Western approach which

Sanyo folding travel iron 1972 This neat travelling iron shows the Japanese designers' gift for compactness at its best. Its bright colour makes it a 'life-style' object *par excellence.*

**Sony TR610
transistor radio 1958**
The Sony Corporation
was the first to produce
an especially small radio
that could fit into a
pocket. Miniaturization
proved, in fact, to be one
of Japan's strengths in
electronic goods in the
1960s and 1970s.

was based on the furniture traditions that influenced the design of early European and American domestic electronic goods. The first Japanese cameras were also careful copies of the German 35 mm Leica, designed by Oscar Barnak, then considered the most advanced example of camera design in the world, while watches imitated more exclusive Swiss examples.

The models that many Japanese electrical and electronic goods of the 1950s copied came from the USA. (Many were, of course, designed with the American market specifically in mind so it was a natural choice.) Countless Japanese designs emerged in the decade inspired, as were their American counterparts, by the chrome decorative details characteristic of the products of Detroit. Like the American models they were based upon, the Japanese goods were 'styled', which meant that the technological components were simply enclosed in a box, the surface of which was then decorated with familiar motifs culled from the American automobile – at the time the most popular of all mass-produced icons. Radios, television sets and refrigerators

were covered with pieces of chrome trim and embellished with shiny control knob details which derived from the 'Cadillac' school of design. This approach constituted a crude form of marketing in which Japanese manufacturers emulated their American counterparts so as to conform to the popular taste of the day.

The growing emphasis upon design in the 1950s in establishment circles had little immediate impact on the majority of Japanese electrical and electronic consumer goods (see chapter 2). They continued to pour out of the factories with an appearance that was determined, for the most part, by technical and/or economic requirements, or with the addition of some 'styling' details. The main emphasis was on producing the greatest possible number of modestly priced, technically sophisticated goods to meet the growing needs of mass markets at home and abroad. In most of these products there was a certain crudeness of line, detail and finish. However, the fact that their appearance was heavily influenced by the technology was a plus rather than a minus, for much of their appeal lay in the way they exhibited

Sharp hand-held calculators 1980s The Sharp Company put a great deal of effort into producing ever smaller and slimmer calculators as a mark of its technical competence. By the 1980s, it had produced one which fitted neatly into the palm of the hand.

technical sophistication, which produced an abundance of overt gadgetry. In turn, this was to develop into a 'high-tech' look which, by the 1970s, had become a Japanese hallmark and was becoming a familiar part of product form internationally. It was visible in the cameras, audio equipment and watches, and came to represent *the* late-twentieth-century aesthetic for high-technology goods.

One company which took a highly self-conscious approach to design was Sony. From its foundation, Sony clearly combined technological innovation with a high level of visual sophistication. Committed from the outset to the progressive idea of developing new audio products for the home which could be categorized as pieces of 'equipment' rather than, more conventionally, as items of furniture, in 1950 Sony produced the first Japanese tape-recorder. The following year the Corporation fitted it into a suitcase, thereby turning it into a portable model for domestic use. Four years later, borrowing technological know-how from the American Bell Laboratories and the Western Electric Company, the corporation produced the first Japanese transistor radio. By 1957 this had been 'miniaturized' to fit into a pocket, and in 1959 Sony launched the world's first all-transistor television set.

The drive to manufacture ever smaller and increasingly multi-functional domestic electronic products became a major characteristic of Japanese design after the war, representing one tangible way in which technology and design moved closely hand in hand. For many manufacturers the more 'miniature' the product the more sophisticated its technological achievement and the more integrated its form and function. It was a logical direction for

Japanese manufacturers to explore as it combined the requirement to integrate the most sophisticated electronic technology both with the real need to export as large a quantity of goods as possible, and with the limitations imposed by the diminutive size of the average Japanese home. This tendency in Japanese design has reached its peak in recent years with the hand-held calculator, which has now become so thin that it can be manipulated in the palm of the hand or fitted into a wristwatch. This dramatic

Nikon FA camera 1984 Along with Canon, Olympus, Minolta and Pentax, the Nikon Company is known for the high level of technical excellence in its products. Modelled originally on the German Leica, by the 1970s, the Japanese camera had evolved an aesthetic which stressed technical sophistication.

piece of engineering virtuosity has brought to a logical end the strand of post-war Japanese product design which has stressed the subservience of aesthetics to technological prowess. The main problem associated with the miniature product in market terms is that its small size gives it little impact when displayed at point of sale. The only answer was for marketing departments to emphasize its smallness and lightness, well exemplified by Sony's elegant range of televisions from the Trinitron models to the slim 'Profeel' design.

While these goods emphasized the expressive and innately mysterious functions of high-technology products through visual simplification, another, parallel, and more widely disseminated tendency in Japanese design stressed visual complexity. By the 1970s this had resulted in a 'neo-baroque' image for high-technology goods which became associated exclusively with Japan. While the minimal approach had much in common with the sophisticated technological aesthetic developed in Germany and based on Modern Movement principles, the Japanese 'high-tech' look was native-born and quickly became much more typical of Japanese products as they were known internationally in the 1960s and 1970s. Thus, Japanese post-war electronic goods represented both aspects of Japanese aesthetics – the austere *and* the flamboyant.

The 'high-tech' look was the designers' response to a complex problem. Once products were no longer considered as items of furniture, interior décor, or formal sculpture, but as pieces of equipment, the constraints imposed by high-technology mass-manufacturing methods would result in little more than sheet metal boxes housing complex components. A cheap way of providing visual interest in these anonymous boxes was to focus on the design details of the control knobs and dials, and to add graphics to the fascias

Sony Profeel television 1987 The design of the 1987 model of Sony's slim Profeel television set shows the corporation's continued commitment to visual elegance and minimalism.

Sharp compact disc cassette player 1980s
One of the tendencies in the design of Japanese electronic goods has been to combine individual, miniaturized pieces of equipment into a multi-functional, complex assemblage of items.

Yamaha TC 800 cassette deck 1980s
In looking for a sophisticated design for this deck, Yamaha went to Mario Bellini, best known for his wedge-shaped typewriters designed for Olivetti.

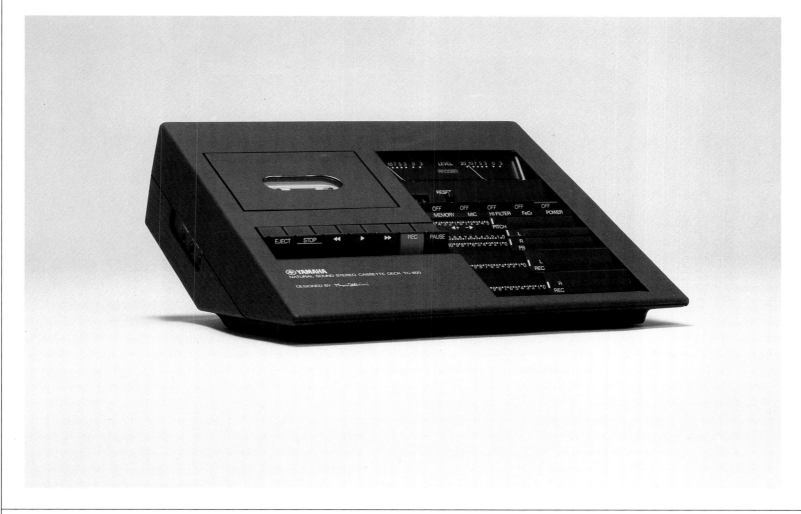

of such objects as cassette tape systems, stereo hi-fi systems, portable radios, and, a little later, compact disc players and video recorders. Far from simplifying them or making them 'user-friendly' by making the mechanisms appear easy to operate, Japanese manufacturers opted for a more complex look which aimed to persuade consumers that in purchasing this highly complicated piece of technology they had been offered real 'value for money'. The approach flattered consumers by implying that they had a high level of intelligence in being able to understand the machine, instead of having everything spelled out for them. It was a clever piece of marketing, and design teams spent their time working on control panels and the details of products to meet the requirements of the marketing managers. Liquid crystal displays and electro-luminescent devices increased the look

of technological sophistication and impressivness. By the early 1970s Japanese audio and video equipment, with its complicated satin-finished chrome fascias, could be found in homes throughout the world, often banked up in piles and resembling the control consoles of space rockets. Japanese hi-fi systems brought the imagery of space and military research into the domestic environment. The tendency to combine functions, such as tape-recording and record-playing, into single units also became increasingly widespread in the 1970s and soon the concept of housing discrete functions in single shells had become obsolete. Miniature components were clustered together to create a visual impact through the sum of the parts.

By the end of the 1970s, this image of technological wizardry had helped Japanese electronic goods achieve a

Radian hi-fi system 1983 This all-black hi-fi system, with its complex control panel and graphic details, epitomizes the aggressive, 'masculine' high-tech look that characterized so many Japanese electronic goods in the 1970s and 1980s.

mass-market presence around the globe. A corporate approach to design had developed, where designers worked as a team within the company. Although Japanese design practice derived from the commercial American approach, the Americans favoured independent industrial design consultants, while Japanese companies retained a preference for the anonymous, in-house designer who remained, at all times, a 'company man'. The products of manufacturing concerns such as Sony, Sharp, Toshiba, Hitachi and others were, and are, designed by members of a design team rather than individual 'stars'. Moreover, these teams are usually part of their company's marketing division, and design is subservient to marketing.

In recent years there has been an increasing emphasis, within product design, on the concept of 'cultural variation'.

Design is a variable, responsible primarily for linking a particular product with a particular market, or with one sector of it. This is in sharp contrast with the practice in the immediate post-war years when the designer's task was simply one of styling standardized products. A good example of this is the Ricoh Company, originally camera manufacturers but now involved primarily with photocopying machinery and other pieces of automated office equipment. It has moved its design emphasis from the practice of styling standardized products to finding a more flexible approach in answer to a more diverse and sophisticated market.

At the same time, the manufacturing process has moved from a system of mass production to providing 'many versions in small lots' made possible by an increased use of

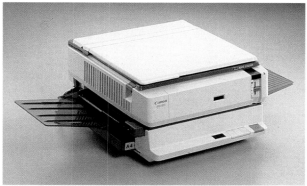

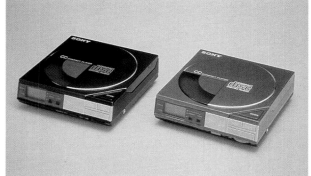

Canon mini-copier PC20 1983 Another example of Japanese miniaturization, the mini-copier was designed to fit into a domestic space as well as an office environment.

Sony compact disc player D50 1985 Sony perfected the compact disc system and designed its players in line with its commitment to neat, minimal, design.

Sharp portable radio-cassette player 1980s Sharp's multi-functional, high-tech complex-looking assemblage is in fact still just compact enough to be carried by hand.

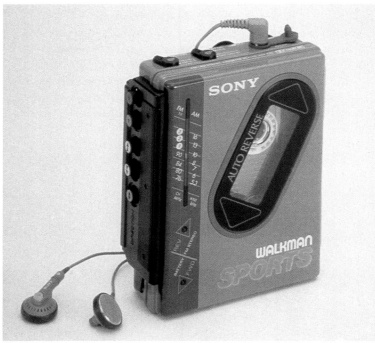

Sony Walkman 'Sport' models WM75 and WMF75 1985
Once the idea of Sony's portable mini cassette player had proved successful, the corporation produced it in a range of 'life-style' colours. These items contrasted dramatically with the stark minimalism of many of Sony's products.

Sharp 'Turbine W' vacuum cleaner 1983
This compact domestic vacuum cleaner is produced in a range of colours to fit a domestic interior setting.

Sharp colour video camera Committed to producing electronic goods based on advanced technology, Sharp designed its video camera in a manner that could fit into either a domestic or a professional situation.

automatic techniques in the production process. The Ricoh Company defines its present design philosophy as being one of providing a 'comfortable relationship between man and machine'. (The formulation of a specific philosophy for its approach to design is also characteristic of the Japanese electronics industry.) The development of product variation became more widespread in the early 1980s. As the youth market became increasingly important in Japan, the association of electrical and electronic goods with a technological utopia based upon complexity, mystification, seriousness and sophistication gave way to the idea of designed artefacts reflecting the values of youthfulness, fun and life-style in general. Increasingly, designers have seen themselves in a social, rather than an exclusively manufacturing, context. The more widespread use of plastics instead of metal, has helped to produce a rounded look and a greater range of colours, reflecting the character and potential of plastic processes. Bright colours were first used for Japanese products in this area in the early 1980s, replacing the ubiquitous black and chrome of the late 1970s. The use first of red and green and subsequently pastel shades served to dilute the highly mechanistic imagery of earlier products and to introduce a new humanism. Once again, the inspiration for this change came from abroad – in this case the Post-Modern furniture and buildings produced by avant-garde Italian designers, and American architects. Not surprisingly, the introduction of these new colours was modified by specifically Japanese values, in this case the rules of colour symbolism.

The Japanese 'life-style' product *par excellence* is, without doubt, Sony's 'Walkman' personal portable stereo tape-cassette player, complete with earphones. The product concept is attributed to Mr Morita himself, as a way to relieve the boredom of trans-Atlantic air travel. It was tested on a group of teenagers, all of whom instantly began to dance as they listened to it. This persuaded Sony that they had a marketable product on their hands. In keeping with its young 'pop' image the Walkman was soon available in red and, for the waterproof sports version, bright yellow, followed, the next year, by a wide range of fashion colours.

On the whole, however, Sony has resisted moving away from the 'classical' aesthetic it developed in the late 1970s and many of its 1980s products retained the familiar black and chrome look. It has remained, essentially, conservative in its design approach, concentrating its efforts on technological research and pioneering such innovative products as the 'Watchman' TV and the 'Mavica' filmless video camera. In contrast, numerous other manufacturers in this area, among them Sharp, Toshiba and National, have leapt enthusiastically into the area of 'life-style' goods,

Toshiba 'Walky' cassette player 1983
This group of tape players is available in a range of fashion colours to suit the life-styles of the teenage market at which they were aimed.

Minolta 7000 AF, 1985; Olympus XA2 1981; Canon T50 1986; and Fujica 'Picpal' 1983 *(clockwise)* A range of Japanese cameras from the 1980s representing a spectrum from the highly serious Minolta and Canon, designed for the expert, to the compact Olympus, designed by Kenji Ekuan of GK Associates which is much simpler to use, and the 'fun' Fujica camera which produces snapshots with little effort from the photographer. The first three designs have won awards at home and abroad.

producing a wide range of highly fashionable items which appeal to the young. In the area of domestic appliances, Sharp has produced a range of pastel-coloured products – including a rice-cooker and a microwave oven, pictured in an advertising brochure alongside a young girl dressed in the same colours.

In the mid-1980s, household gadgets have become as symbolically linked with life-style as fashion clothing had always been, simply through the appropriation of certain colours. A characteristic of the fashion style of the 1980s, and another reason for introducing pastel shades into a wide spectrum of goods from washing machines to television sets, was the strong alliance of products with the stylistic revival of 1950s American culture, a phenomenon which in Japan has permeated a wide range of cultural artefacts aimed at the youth market. Even cameras have moved away from black to bright colours, as demonstrated by Canon's range of 'Snappy' instamatic models. As always, this is combined with technological innovation, in this case the fully automatic self-focusing camera. To integrate these products into the

general home environment, advertisements portrayed them alongside pieces of fashionable Italian furniture and other life-style accoutrements. In 1985 such products as National's pink radio, evocatively named 'Holiday', were available alongside Sharp's 'Hi-cooker' (manufactured in white, pink, yellow, turquoise and burgundy), Sanyo's baby-blue 'Taro' vacuum cleaner, and Toshiba's pastel-coloured alarm clocks and hair-dryers.

Not surprisingly, Japan has been the first country to experiment commercially with a Post-Modern approach to product design. While this movement had been steadily gaining ground in architecture and interior and furniture design, no other country had been sufficiently advanced in its automated manufacturing technology to be able to transfer it into product design since, traditionally, the high cost of investment in tooling has made such experimentation impossible. Japan's high level of automation and 'flexible specialization' (see chapter 2) has enabled it to introduce product variation quite easily into the mass manufacture of, say, a microwave oven or a piece of

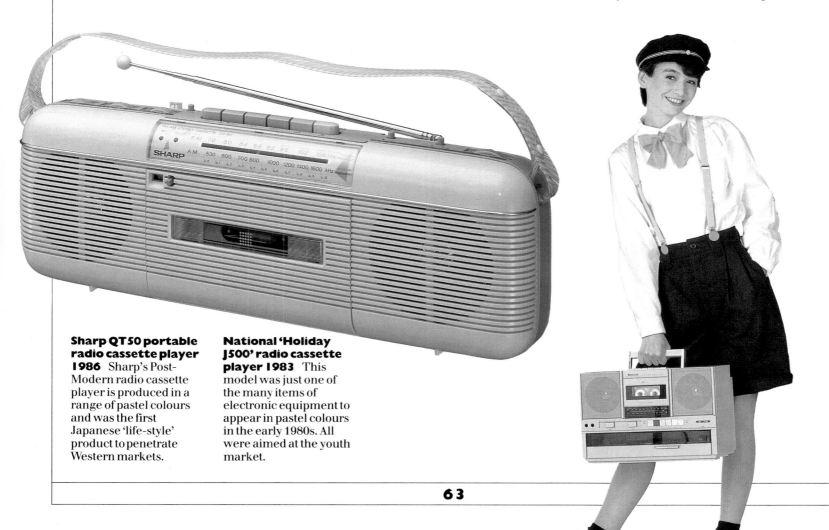

Sharp QT50 portable radio cassette player 1986 Sharp's Post-Modern radio cassette player is produced in a range of pastel colours and was the first Japanese 'life-style' product to penetrate Western markets.

National 'Holiday J500' radio cassette player 1983 This model was just one of the many items of electronic equipment to appear in pastel colours in the early 1980s. All were aimed at the youth market.

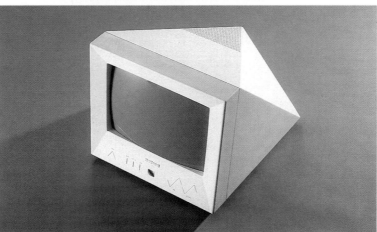

**National Panasonic
'Future Design' series 1985**
These highly innovative
Post-Modern designs for
television sets mark a radical
rejection of the high- tech
aesthetic.

audio equipment. The technological success of Japanese manufacturers contributed to their unique position to cater for changing tastes and fashions in the styling of electrical goods.

The most radical rejection of the 'high-tech' aesthetic and attempt to integrate Post-Modern ideas into product design came in 1985 with National Panasonic's prototype 'Future Design' series of appliances – among them a toaster, a juice-mixer, an egg-cooker and a coffee-machine. National Panasonic not only used vivid colours such as orange, yellow, lilac and green, but also proposed a completely new imagery for such appliances. This imagery has more in common with

children's wooden or plastic toys than with the familiar 'high-tech' metal shapes. The idea that product design was serious, high-minded and middle-aged had been undermined once and for all.

Japan now leads the world, not only in technological research where work in advanced electronics, robotics, and into 'alternative' power sources dominate the field, but also in marketing and product design. By a process of, first imitating, and subsequently improving on the work of their foreign competitors, Japanese manufacturers of electrical and electronic goods have now overtaken them and have produced objects which match the cultural variety that has

**National Panasonic
'Future Design' series 1985**
A range of prototype designs
for domestic appliances, these
brightly coloured artefacts
show the strong 'life-style'
emphasis of so many Japanese
electronic goods of the 1980s.

been described as the key characteristics of our 'Post-Modern society'. Their success lies not only in experimentation but in actually manufacturing the goods envisaged.

Japan now produces, and consumes, an enormous amount of high-technology products. While in the years immediately following 1945 that advanced technology was packaged in a fairly crude way, the level of sophistication of the design of Japanese electrical and electronic goods is now as good as or better than its Western counterparts. Few of these products have, on the surface at least, any obvious links with Japanese craft-based aesthetic traditions. None

the less, these links do exist; they are visible in Japan's continued ability to embrace change, in its openness to foreign influences but at the same time its determination to bring to those influences something of its cultural past, and in its almost obsessive interest in quality, whether of technology or design. In the area of high-technology goods, Japan has created its own concept of 'design' which, in the end, has little in common with Western definitions of the term. It represents a complete synthesis of design technology and marketing and has undoubtedly been one of the key factors in Japan's economic success of the post-war years.

Chapter 4

Automotive products

In no other area of contemporary production has Japan achieved a greater reputation for its manufacturing ability, low costing and advanced technology than in that of transportation. At the same time, the concept has been established, and still lingers, that although they are undoubtedly good value for money and highly reliable machines, the design of Japanese cars (when compared with their more sophisticated European counterparts) leaves much to be desired. Although this situation is rapidly changing, and many Japanese cars of the 1980s have impressed foreign buyers with their attention to visual detail and their innovative design features, the fact remains that designers are dealing with a product that has very little affinity with traditional Japanese aesthetic values. In the absence of this frame of reference, the Japanese have tended to depend almost entirely upon American and European models for visual inspiration. For this reason, Japan has taken longer to develop a modern automobile design movement of its own and has tended, instead, to employ the 'copying' principle somewhat indiscriminately. In spite of this, there are many specifically 'Japanese' characteristics in the cars that have emerged from Japan since the 1950s. There are also signs that this formative period of Japanese transport design is coming to an end. A growing sense of maturity is evident in many of Japan's designs of the 1980s and the feeling is emerging that the country is looking more frequently within itself for ideas, rather than copying foreign designs. This is in part due to the expanding domestic market. Although the export market is still important to Japanese manufacturers, now that practically everyone in Japan has a car, models are being produced to meet Japanese requirements. Hence the small, efficient town cars, ideally suited to the Japanese urban environment of the 1980s.

Unlike graphic and clothing design, and architecture – all of which have long, well-defined traditions within Japanese culture – the automobile only arrived in Japan after the Kanto earthquake of 1923. The earthquake destroyed Tokyo's railway and tramway (streetcar) systems, leaving the way open for foreign car manufacturers to flood the Japanese transport market. Ford exported 1,000 buses to Japan at that time and by 1925 both they and General Motors had established assembly plants in Japan. This take-over by the large-scale American concerns led to complete domination by the USA in the area of transportation and by 1929 these two American companies accounted for 85 per cent of the entire market.

Neither the Japanese zaibatsus (trading companies) nor the government had shown any interest in developing an indigenous automotive industry until the early 1930s. After

Toyota A1 1935 and Roadster 1933 The A1 *(above)* was directly influenced by the streamlined forms of Chrysler's Airflow model of 1934. The roadster *(right)* was a much more conservative model although there were signs of visual integration – the rear wheel, for example – in its design.

**Nissan Datsun
1932** A fairly
unsophisticated model
in design terms, this car
closely resembled
contemporary
automobiles produced
in Europe and the USA,
in particular Henry
Ford's model T.

that, largely as a result of the need for transport for the military initiative in China in 1937, the government's attitude began to change and by 1946 a programme was being implemented of forcing American industry out and of encouraging native industry. The earliest companies to move into this new area were Nissan (originally Jidosha Seizo) and Toyota, an offshoot of Toyoda, a manufacturer of textile machinery. The USA, inevitably, had an enormous influence on Japanese automobile design in its early phases. While Nissan's early models – the Datsuns Type 12 and Type 13 of 1932 and 1934 respectively – were small cars, rather old-fashioned in design and highly reminiscent of Ford's model T, Toyota took a more progressive American model, the ill-fated streamlined Chrysler Airflow of 1934, as the source of inspiration for its first car, the A1, produced in 1935. Two years later it had been developed into a production model and it subsequently provided the basis for all Toyota's designs in the 1940s.

Up until that time the majority of Japanese cars and trucks (more of the latter in fact being produced than of the former) were supplied to the army or to the government. It was not until the early 1960s that the concept of a passenger car became common currency for the average Japanese family.

The reconstruction of Japan's automobile industry after the Second World War (the war had practically destroyed it in its infancy) was in the hands of three major manufacturers, Nissan, Toyota and Mitsubishi – the last a transport division of the large zaibatsu. By 1949, production was back to the

1941 level of 50,000 units, of which only 12,000 were passenger cars. A major call on jeep-type vehicles and military trucks came at the time of the Korean War in 1952. MITI introduced a 'Basic Policy for the Introduction of Foreign Investment into Japan's Passenger Car Industry' which actually forbade the importation of foreign models for the first time, thereby putting pressure on the Japanese industry to supply the country's needs.

Nissan Datsun 110 1955 The appearance of Nissan's first post-war automobile for the domestic market *(above left)* owed a great deal to contemporary British models, such as the Hillman.

Nissan Fairlady 2000 1963 The form of the Fairlady sports car *(above)* was reminiscent of sleek Italian designs from the period. It showed a sophistication of line unusual in Japanese automobiles at that early date.

Suzuki Suzulight SL 1957 Previously motorcycle manufacturers, the Suzuki Company, like Honda, moved, in the 1950s, into small cars for the domestic market. This model was one of their first.

Honda S800M 1966
Although Honda made
its name, in the 1950s,
with its designs for
motor-scooters and
motorcycles, by the 1960s
it had moved into small
car production. The
styling of this compact
sports model from the
middle of the decade
owed a visual debt to
British examples.

In spite of the fact that the American industry no longer dominated the Japanese transport market, American, and to a lesser extent, British design still provided models for Japanese manufacturers. In 1955 Nissan, for instance, launched its Datsun A110 series, a chunky compact car with an essentially unified body-shell which, in its simplicity, was reminiscent of both British and American models. By 1959 this had developed into an early model of one of the company's best-known cars, the Bluebird, which remained in production, albeit with countless modifications, into the 1970s. Nissan's other major breakthroughs of the late 1950s and early 1960s included the Cedric, which was launched in 1960 as the company's first medium-sized passenger car, and included such novel features for Japan as vertically arranged dual headlights and a wrap-around windshield. Modifications were made to the car through the 1960s; the 1965 model was a joint creation of Pininfarina and Nissan, and the 1968 version, for the first time, incorporated forceful

and expressive American styling details, such as the chrome trim on the doors and the bumpers (fenders). As most Japanese cars produced for the domestic market were aimed at the businessman (the new élite of Japanese society), manufacturers were keen to increase the size of their products (or at least give the illusion of size) and add features which conveyed 'social status'. Another highly successful Nissan car, the 'prestige' Gloria, was launched in 1959. It developed from resembling the rather dumpy British Hillman to, in the mid-1960s, emulating the more extravagant American style, thereby exhibiting even more 'status appeal'.

Toyota's most important passenger car of the early years was the Crown, launched in 1955 (see page 37). It was the success of this car which prompted Nissan to launch the Cedric as a direct competitor. The Crown was a substantial car, developed for official and formal use but also utilized as a taxi-cab as well as for more general purposes. In its chrome trim, and hoods over the headlamps, it also owed a debt both to Britain's Hillman and to American styling as it evolved through the 1950s and early 1960s. In the second half of the 1960s, increased affluence in Japan meant that a larger proportion of the population was acquiring bigger cars for private use and the Crown, along with its imitators, became a definite status symbol.

Until the late 1960s, Japanese cars had fallen into two main types – the substantial formal car, usually chauffeur driven, and the smaller family-owned car which came into being during the course of the 1950s. Only the most compact models were generally privately owned. This particular market was catered for by mini-cars, manufactured by companies which had started out producing motorcycles. Among the models produced in these years were Suzuki's Suzulight (marketed as the Suzulite in the USA) of 1957, Subaru's model 360 of 1958 (a little bubble-car which drew

heavily on European examples), and Mazda's R360 of 1960. In 1960, Toyota also realized the potential of the market for smaller cars and produced the compact Publica, so-named because it went on sale to the general public. Simple in design and essentially European in flavour, it remained a popular car through the 1960s and early 1970s.

It was during this period that the Japanese automobile industry really started to gain ground. As Sol Saunders has written in his account of the Honda company, 'Japan entered the 1960s with a production of less than a hundred thousand cars annually but arrived at the end of the decade as the second largest producer in the world [after the US].'[1] The success of the industry resulted both from its ability to supply the demand of the ever-expanding home market and from its aggressive policy towards exporting its production. The stylistic dependence on foreign models was largely a result of the need to compete with them in their own market

Toyota 1000 Prototype 1956 The design for Toyota's little utility 1000 model was initiated in 1954. Designed for private use in towns, it was a revolutionary car when it appeared, unlike anything the company had produced before.

Nissan Datsun truck 1951 The truck version of the most basic Datsun model was a highly compact and utilitarian design.

places. By the early 1970s many Japanese cars competed favourably due, primarily, to the combination of their low cost, their high technical efficiency, and their high-technology extras: design, generally, was considered less important than price in the mass market.

One Japanese automobile company which has strongly emphasized design throughout the post-war period is Honda. It remains the exception on a number of fronts, in particular through its continued independence from the large trading companies and from links with American companies. (This contrasts sharply with the policies of Mitsubishi and Isuzu, for instance, which have developed rapports with Chrysler and General Motors respectively.)

The Honda Motor Company was established in 1946, and devoted its energies initially to the development of a motorcycle which would be appropriate to the Japanese life-style. The earliest models of 1948 were very simple,

involving only the addition of a motor to a conventional bicycle frame. But the Dream cycle of 1959 moved more in the direction of a light motorcycle, and provided the basis of a line of designs which stretched into the 1970s. It helped to give Japan a significant reputation for production in this field in the post-war period, and put the longer established British industry out of business in the process.

Honda's other post-war experiments included the Juno scooter – a streamlined version of an Italian formula – but its greatest success lay in the development of the step-through 50cc Super-Cub (marketed as the Supercab in the USA) motorcycle which was designed with Japan's narrow urban alleys and tracks through paddy fields in mind. Not only did the Super-Cub succeed in winning a substantial Japanese market, it also managed, with the help of a number of extensive and sophisticated marketing campaigns, to make a significant mark in the USA (and, to a lesser extent, in

Subaru 360 1958
Probably the most visually interesting of the Japanese mini-cars of the 1950s, the Subaru was essentially a hybrid, inspired by the small cars produced by both Fiat and Renault in that decade.

Toyota Crown RS 1955 The first example of Toyota's more substantial automobile, the Crown owed its appearance to American styling as well as to British models.

Honda Super-Cub motorcycle 1958
Honda's little 50cc step-through bike provided an alternative image to that of the highly styled Italian Vespa, for low-powered two-wheel transport.

Honda Juno motor-scooter Type K 1954 Honda's first attempt at a motor-scooter was a strange space-age object combining American styling with Italian scooter design.

Yamaha YA1 motorcycle 1955 One of Yamaha's early successes in motorcycle manufacture, the YA1 shows the company's early commitment to design.

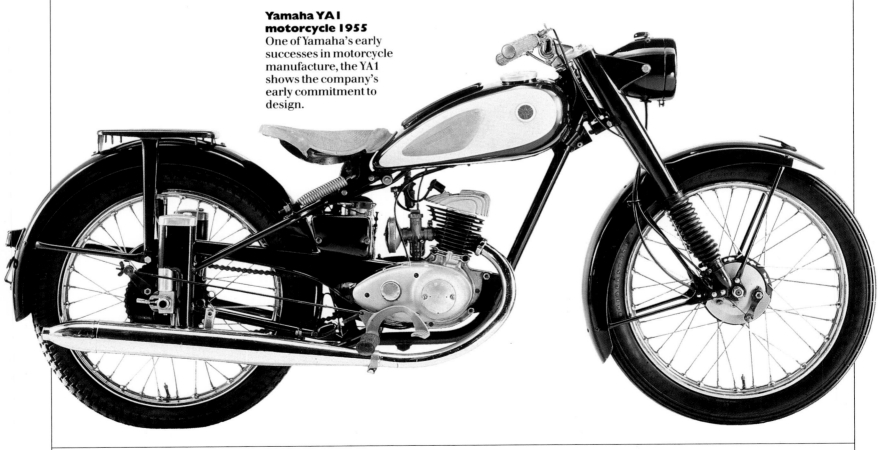

Europe). This was Soichiro Honda's greatest achievement: to be able to sell a small, funny-looking motorcycle in a country where motorcycles were inextricably linked with the image of Marlon Brando, grease and black leather. The Super-Cub's appeal lay in its simple utilitarian appearance, and its lack of additional 'styling' details. This pared-down

functionalism was responsible for the model's popularity among older and younger age groups.

The story of the success of the Japanese motorcycle industry is an important part of the Japanese economic post-war success story. In addition to Honda, the Suzuki, Kawasaki and Yamaha companies also played an important

Honda 'Dream' motorcycle 1949 The company's first motorcycle designs were fairly primitive, looking more like motorized bicycles than the aggressive machines that they were to become later.

Honda Cub Type F 1952 This is an early, very basic version of what was to become Honda's step-through motorcycle.

Honda Model A motorcycle 1947 One of the first Honda motorcyles, this primitive design is little more than a motor attached to a conventional bicycle frame.

part in securing enormous international respect for the post-war Japanese motorcycle industry. As with the early cars, however, the models' appeal in foreign markets lay more in their level of technological innovation and low cost than in their design.

Yahama was an exception, however. The company began by producing quality organs in 1897 but diversified into motorcycles after the war, because of its engineering facilities. From the beginning the company's president, Kaichi Kawakami, considered design to be an important element within manufacturing and from 1957 onwards worked in conjunction with GK Industrial Design Associates. This relationship lasted for many years, and earned Yamaha a high reputation for its design achievements both in motorcycles, and in products it diversified into, such as the

well-known tape-deck designed by the Italian Mario Bellini (see page 57).

The success that Honda achieved with its little motorcycle in the USA was followed up by its experience in car manufacturing. Following on the heels of the other motorcycle producers, such as Suzuki, Subaru and Yahama, who had moved successfully into the mini-car market, Honda launched the N360 model in 1967. Inspired by the Austin Mini, this car appealed strongly to the new, increasingly affluent youth market in Japan and set a precedent for the high level of design in the Japanese mini-cars which followed it. This high standard was both established and sustained by Honda through the production, in 1970, of its Z series, with its novel rear styling; in 1971 of its Life series; and in 1972 the well-known Civic – which more

Toyota Corona 1500 Deluxe 1966 The Corona aped American executive cars from this period. Prestige rather than 'good design' was the order of the day.

Nissan Sunny 1000 1966 The Nissan Company's cars from the mid-1960s were, on the whole, prestige saloon models which lacked any charisma in design. The Sunny 1000 was a basic model, the result of technological and economic expediency rather than design expertise.

Honda N360 1967 Honda's mini-car followed on the heels of versions of the same concept pioneered in the previous decade by, among others, Suzuki and Subaru.

than any other model helped put Honda on the international automobile map. Finally, after a gap of ten years, in 1982 Honda produced the little City model which, with its dramatically sloping front and high headroom, constituted one of the major design breakthroughs of the 1980s.

In addition to these impressive series of mini-car models, Honda has also ventured into the larger two-volume and three-volume automobile sectors, producing, yet again, some of Japan's most sophisticated designs, among them the visually controlled and well-thought-out Accord and Prelude models. The design director responsible for both these cars, and for the Civic, was Hiroshi Kizawa. From the beginning the Honda Company was committed to the idea of high quality. As early as 1951, Soichiro Honda is reported to have said that, 'if Japanese technology were good and Japanese

products were high in quality, then the Japanese would not have to import foreign-made products . . . I resolved to prove that high-quality goods know no national boundaries'.[2]

Two factors dominated Japanese car production in the 1970s – the oil crisis and the growth of the prestige car for the owner-driver (rather than company) market. They pulled Japanese cars in two opposing directions. The oil crisis of 1973 meant a sudden interest in the energy-saving features of transport, resulting in a series of compact 'Best Efficiency Technology' models. The growth of the owner-driver market encouraged a renewed move into the area of high-class, status cars. Both tendencies co-existed through the 1970s with different results for Japanese automobile design.

In the area of status cars, countless models emerged from the main manufacturers – Nissan, Toyota, Honda, Daihatsu

Honda 600Z Honda's little 600 model followed the design trends of the other compact cars which preceded it. Its forms were echoed in the highly successful Honda Civic.

Honda Civic 1972 The Civic was the first of the Japanese small cars to make an impact on the Western market. It was designed with more attention to visual detail than most of its Japanese contemporaries and for the first time caused the West to see Japan as a source of design – as well as technological – expertise in the area of automobiles.

Suzuki CV1 1982
Shown at the Tokyo motor show, this novel little three-wheeler demonstrated Japan's preoccupation with compactness in the post-oil-crisis years of the early 1980s.

Daihatsu Charade
Developed in the 1970s, the Charade was modelled on European examples; more attention was paid to visual detail than had been usual in the past.

and Mitsubishi – who vied with one another for the greatest share of the market. Variations on Toyota's Corona, Corolla, and Carina models sat beside Nissan's Sunny, Laurel, Cedric and Gloria (among others), with differences in appearance becoming increasingly difficult to distinguish. A down-to-earth and conservative approach characterized these cars. One writer, in *Car Styling* magazine – the leading voice of Japan's automobile industry – in describing Nissan's Gloria of 1977, remarked that it was intended for the executives of small businesses and that it could not, therefore, 'gamble on a futuristic design'.[3] By 1980, critics writing in the same magazine were making such comments as 'Cars from Japan have initially nothing to offer in the way of taste or charm'; that 'Japanese cars all look the same'; and that they were 'all copied from rival models'.[4] Even many of the smaller, economy, two-volume, hatchback cars – among them Mitsubishi's 1978 Mirage (marketed as the Colt in the USA)

and Daihatsu's Charade of the same year – clearly owed much to Giorgio Giugiaro's Volkswagen Golf (Rabbit) which, in the early 1970s, had provided the international model for that class of car.

The main reason usually given for Japan's generally low level of design innovation in the early post-war years was the presence of an ever-expanding domestic market which was both, in one writer's words, 'potentially bottomless and immature'.[5] The willingness of this new and affluent market to buy whatever was presented to it gave manufacturers absolute control over design. Models, consequently, were produced to the cheapest possible technological specification, which led to indiscriminate styling.

By the late 1970s the growing problems of manufacturing (primarily the oil crisis, and the recession) and the increasing sophistication of the domestic market combined to create a need for more thought in design. One

Toyota Soarer
Modelled on 'status' European cars, the Soarer is one of the luxury cars that have emerged from Japan in recent years.

Honda Spacy 1982
Honda pioneered the return to the motor-scooter in the 1980s. The main design aim was to achieve a much more high-technology image for the scooter.

Mazda Cosmo 1981
Another of the prestige cars to come out of Japan in the 1980s, the Cosmo is modelled on luxury, high-quality European cars like the German Mercedes and Audi ranges.

commentator pointed out that, 'Unlike their European counterparts the Japanese did not create a distinct car design outlook,'[6] but by the late 1970s discussions of 'taste and individuality' had become much more frequent. A number of initiatives, including the Nissan Company setting up its Datsun US Design Center in California, and increasing numbers of young Japanese automobile designers being sent abroad to study design (many of them at the Art Center School in Los Angeles), were aimed at helping to fill the 'design gap'. It was quite quickly realized that what was important was less close competition between similarly styled products, and the adoption of what was described as a 'multiple-angle approach to design'.[7]

By the 1980s, these moves were beginning to show results and it became possible to talk about a 'design movement' in the Japanese automobile world. While the large prestige cars continued to flow off the production lines (many of them

still owing a great deal to the large German status cars such as Mercedes, Audi and BMW), other, more varied models also appeared to appeal to different sectors of the market. In the 'kei' (small) car sector (which had a greater international impact in Europe than in the USA), for instance, Mitsubishi's Minica of 1981, Subaru's Rex of the same year, and Suzuki's Fronte conveyed a new sense of confidence in design expertise, while Honda's City of the following year provided a whole new image for the compact, town car. Other small cars which began to demonstrate the same originality in design, and lack of stylistic dependence on European models included Nissan's Pulsar, Toyota's Tercel and Suzuki's Cervo. A writer in a 1983 edition of *Car Styling* exclaimed, when describing this particular range of cars, that, 'It's just been in the last twelve months that the domestic market for popular economy cars has really come alive.' The design of these models now matched their technological excellence.[8]

Toyota Master Ace Surf 4WD Grand Saloon 1985 One of the most popular 'life-style' concepts for family driving in the mid-1980s was epitomized by this 1985 version of Toyota's earlier Hi-Ace wagon. Its all-important symbolic associations spanned space travel to the 'sporting life'.

Honda CBR 750 1986 By the mid-1980s Japanese motorcycles had evolved an aggressive, masculine, space-age image all of their own. Their technological sophistication matched their visual slickness.

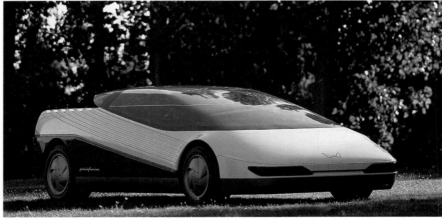

Honda HP-X 1984 The HP-X is one of the most dramatic concept cars of the mid-1980s. Tokyo motor shows of this period all boasted such futuristic models as a mark of Japan's wish to appear 'up-to-date'.

Honda City GG 1986
More than any other contemporary Japanese car, Honda's little City, with its high roof and dramatically pitched bonnet, shows that finally Japan's reliance on Western design has been broken and Japanese automotive design has come of age.

In addition to the renewed sense of life in the small car range, a vast number of novelty cars also appeared in the early 1980s destined to meet the varied needs of the young, highly fashion-conscious market. Toyota's new 4WD Sprinter of 1982, for instance, was described in advertising literature as a natural appendage to the casual life-style that is characterized by 'blue jeans, fishing jackets and Walkmans',[9] and marks the culmination of the trend away from production orientation to consumer orientation. Japanese manufacturers were planning products, and designing them, for specific life-styles.

A much greater sense of sophistication pervaded the marketing aspect of these essentially fashion-oriented cars and this was inevitably reflected in their designs. One such 'novelty' design from 1982, Nissan's Prairie, which could accommodate a family of eight, for example, was designed by Itaru Sugino, a recent graduate from the Art Center School in Pasadena. Mitsubishi quickly introduced its Chariot model, described as a 'super-space' wagon to compete with it and Toyota launched its Space Cruiser, described as a 'car for the large family on the move', a little later.

While what is described as the 'speciality' market had found a place on the periphery of the Japanese automobile world since the mid-1960s – Toyota's Celica of 1970 is a key example – renewed enthusiasm has gone into catering for it within the pluralistic atmosphere of the 1980s. The experimental 'concept' car has also become increasingly popular at the annual Tokyo motor shows, which were instigated in the early 1980s. At the 1984 show, for instance, Nissan, Mazda and Toyota all presented 'concept' models.

Toyota's TAC3, 'a jeep-type', was described as a 'pleasure tool for the younger driver'.[10] Honda still leads the way, however, in design and, in 1985 the company presented the prototype of the Studio HP-X, a sports car designed by the Italian Pininfarina studio. That Honda should go to the acknowledged world leaders in car design is indicative of the new Japanese awareness of the importance of design. Sergio Pininfarina's son Paolo had, moreover, been at Honda's Research and Development Department for a year's training.

The area of transport design is the most difficult to relate to traditional Japanese cultural values as the product was so clearly imported wholesale from the West. Many of the characteristics of Japanese cars in the 1960s and 1970s derived, however, from the problem of approaching this complex, high-technology object from a Japanese perspective. The Japanese love of rectilinearity has already been mentioned, as has the tendency to concentrate on visual details rather than overall form. These preconceptions made it difficult for Japanese car designers to find a comfortable starting point for the development of an indigenous car aesthetic. Instead, they concentrated on what they did best in the post-war years – highly efficient and cost-effective mass production, the prominence of advanced technological details in products, and intensive marketing. In all these areas the Japanese car industry has succeeded and, as a result, Japanese models can now be found everywhere, competing with models from other countries on price, on efficiency and, above all, for their high-technology extras. What has happened in recent years is that they have started to compete in design too.

Chapter 5

Architecture

*'The one country which seems to have found a
satisfactory modern architectural idiom is Japan'*[1]

In architecture, more than in any other design area, the post-war period in Japan has been characterized by a re-importation of many of its own indigenous traditions. After the Second World War, through its dependence upon Western examples, Japan re-absorbed many of the ideals of its own heritage which had been admired, discussed and copied by the European and American promoters of Modernism. Simultaneously, that two-way process of exporting and re-importing brought with it distortions and changes which made modern architecture a new, and largely unrecognizable, phenomenon on Japanese soil. The many elements of modern Western architectural form, including the use of concrete, for example, and the introduction first of medium- and then high-rise structures tended to disguise those attributes which had been culled from Japanese traditional architecture and which had led Western pioneers of modern architecture, such as Frank Lloyd Wright and Bruno Taut, to turn to Japan in search of inspiration.

In spite of this dependence on Western architectural form, the Japanese architects who came to prominence in the energetic years of reconstruction after the war were anxious not to lose links with their own cultural past. There were countless signs, in the concrete metropolises which grew up from the devastation, of the continuity of tradition. The use of the pillar and beam construction method, and of traditional materials in places, the structuring of interiors and their flexibility, and the inclusion of small constructional details in some of the new buildings were indicative of a kind of national consciousness.

The Japanese had already become aware of the avant-garde developments in European and American architecture before the Second World War. When the American architect, Frank Lloyd Wright, built his Imperial Hotel in Tokyo, it had marked a high point in Japan's attempt to import Western architectural ideals. In his earlier Chicago buildings (see chapter 1) Wright had shown his tremendous debt to many traditional Japanese architectural details, including the emphasis upon horizontality, the merging of the inside with the exterior space, and the notion of modularity. Although the hotel was not particularly a monument to Modernism, Wright's presence in Japan served nonetheless as a catalyst in bringing Western ideas to the East. He entrusted its supervision, for example, to Antonin Raymond, a Czech-American who had arrived in Japan in 1919 to work with Wright. In the early 1920s Raymond built as his own residence the first reinforced concrete house in Japan and detailed the concrete frame in

Frank Lloyd Wright, Imperial Hotel Tokyo In his design, Wright combined traditional Japanese constructional features with Western details, such as the furniture, which he designed in a 'Japanese style'.

Le Corbusier, National Museum of Western Art 1959 The only building in Japan designed by Le Corbusier, the museum was completed by his Japanese pupils. The sculpture gallery on the ground floor is shown here.

such a way as to recall traditional Japanese wooden structures. In combining Western and Eastern architectural principles in this way he became an important influence on younger Japanese architects.

This flirtation with the West, and the desire on the part of the Japanese architectural profession to absorb Western Modernism, continued through the inter-war years. Bruno Taut and Charlotte Perriand were both invited to Japan in the 1930s (see pages 30-2) to impart Western architectural ideals and to help the Japanese to integrate them with their own traditions. Architectural magazines, such as *Nippon Architect*, reported Modernist achievements in countries as diverse as Finland, Italy, Austria, the USA and Britain. In turn,

countless young Japanese architectural students travelled to Europe to study at the Bauhaus, and at other educational establishments, and to work in the studios of European Modern masters, among them Le Corbusier.

Through the influence of the later work of Le Corbusier, in particular, Japan's own architectural Modern movement finally crystallized in the years after the Second World War. According to the architectural historian Charles Jencks, 'the explosion in Japan started in the middle fifties with the quick expansion of the economy due in part to the Korean War boom'.[2] The enthusiastic embracing of Modern architecture flourished in that decade due, largely, to the efforts of architects like Junzo Sakakura and Kunio Mayekawa, who

Le Corbusier, National Museum of Western Art 1959 The impact of the European Modern Movement was felt in Japan largely through the influence of Le Corbusier.

Kenzo Tange, Plan for Tokyo 1960 One of the characteristics of Japanese architecture in the 1960s was the desire to construct entire urban environments to replace the cities devastated by the war. Tange's schemes were among the most original.

had worked with Le Corbusier in France and were instrumental in bringing his ideas and idioms to Japan and translating them into Japanese buildings.

In 1937, Sakakura was responsible for the highly praised Japanese pavilion at the Paris exhibition – a hybrid construction which combined traditional Japanese forms, and a tea-room, with overtly Corbusian detailing. In 1951 he applied similar principles to his design for the Modern Art Museum in Kamakura. Eight years later, with Mayekawa and Yoshizaka, he helped complete the National Museum of Western Art, the only structure actually designed by Le Corbusier ever to be built on Japanese soil. In the 1960s Sakakura continued to work on larger scale urban projects such as the Shinjuku station square of 1967.

While the pupils of Le Corbusier made references both to his early and late work, Kenzo Tange, often cited as the father of modern Japanese architecture, quickly began to borrow a language of form, and such ideas as the use of concrete from Le Corbusier's more expressive and organic projects such as the Unités d'Habitation in Marseilles and Chandigarh (India). At the same time, he developed a fusion of Western and Eastern ideals in a burst of building design which, partly on account of the number of projects, and primarily in terms of its innovation, overshadowed all other Japanese architectural achievements in the 1950s and 1960s.

These decades marked a high point in Japan's enthusiasm for and encouragement of new buildings, which were constructed mostly in the devastated cities. The public and

Kenzo Tange, Olympic Gymnasiums 1964 The Tokyo Olympic Games provided an opportunity for Tange to build some of his most important structures. The gymnasiums are a testimony to his growing interest in the organic, expressive late work of Le Corbusier.

Kenzo Tange, Hiroshima Peace Memorial 1955 One of Tange's first public constructions, the Peace Memorial was highly influenced by the 'rational' early work of Le Corbusier.

Kisho Kurokawa, Nagakin Capsule Tower Building 1972 Among the most familiar, to Western eyes, of all of Japan's post-war buildings, the 'capsule' tower introduced into Japanese architecture the Post-Modern practice of using highly symbolic forms. The references were traditional in nature.

Kisho Kurokawa, Helix City 1961 Influenced by the urban fantasy projects of the British 'Archigram' group, the Japanese Metabolists proposed city schemes which grew organically into vast 'mega-structures'.

private projects included housing (sponsored by the Japan Public Housing Corporation), hotels, banks, civic centres, sports and leisure pavilions, universities and museums. Tange received a huge number of commissions – among them, in 1952, City Halls in Tokyo (a government commission), in 1955 the Hiroshima Peace Memorial, and in 1958 the Sogetsu Art Centre. Through these works, he developed a unique combination of the late Corbusian organic aesthetic with such indigenous Japanese features as the interlocking beam method and the post and lintel construction (in his design for the Kurashiki City Hall of 1958-60). It is, however, for his large-scale schemes, including the Boston Bay project of 1959 and the Tokyo Bay project of 1960, and for his designs for the stadiums for the Japanese Olympic Games in 1964, that Tange is best known internationally.

Tange's designs showed for the first time that a Japanese architect could work confidently in a Japanese idiom while still acknowledging the achievements of the Western Modern movement. They also had a great impact on a group of young Japanese architects, collectively referred to as the 'Metabolists', who were to turn the flexible, organic, urban fantasies of the British group, Archigram, into reality on Japanese soil in the 1960s. The rise of the Metabolists, among them Kiyonari Kikutake and Kisho Kurokawa, coincided with the growth of Japanese big business, and their work represented, in many ways, the aspirations of Japanese society in the 1960s. The mechanistic metaphor of

Modernism was rejected and replaced by an organic, biological one – the one favoured much earlier by Frank Lloyd Wright, who had taken his lead from Japan. These architects focused their energies on an all-embracing new vision of the metropolis envisaged in such projects as Kikutake's 'City over the Sea' and Kurokawa's 'Helix City'. Their work assimilated the gains and promises of technological advance and asserted an optimistic vision of the new, urban Japan. That said, however, traditional motifs still appeared, such as the roof forms of Kikutake's 'Tokoen Hotel' and the resemblance of the small boxes, in Kurokawa's 'Nagakin Capsule tower', to tea-ceremony rooms.

Kenzo Tange, Tokyo City Hall Tange's proposal for this high-rise structure brought the European Modern Movement's dream of the 'future city' into the Japanese setting.

Kiyonori Kikutake, Tokoen Hotel 1965 Kikutake's hotel combines a clear display of its structural elements with numerous traditional references, such as the reworking in concrete of a timber constructional technique called 'nuki'.

Kisho Kurokawa, Takara Beautilion 1970 Designed and built for Expo '70 this building clearly displays the Metabolists' use of the biological concept of 'cellular growth'.

By the early 1970s, the concept of 'Post-Metabolist' architecture was being discussed in Japan. Both Tange and Kurokawa (who had worked in Tange's studio) were heavily involved in designing structures for the Expo '70 exhibition which took place in Osaka. Tange evolved a building with a roof which consisted of a huge space-frame made out of steel pipes. Kurokawa's designs for three of the pavilions were to make him one of Japan's best-known 'superstar' architects. While, on the one hand, Expo '70 represented the high point of Metabolism and the zenith of Japan's expansion and faith in technology, it also marked the end of the Japanese profession's faith in the 'high-tech' ethic. Thereafter, the need for a renewed sensibility to challenge the themes of urbanism and consumerism which had dominated many of the achievements of the 1960s became increasingly apparent.

The work of Arata Isozaki, another of the young talents to emerge from Tange's studio, bypassed Metabolism for the most part and proposed instead an aesthetic which combined stylistic eclecticism with a highly self-conscious 'artistic' or 'formalistic' stance. Isozaki's buildings from the 1960s and 1970s utilized traditional, classical and Modernist motifs where appropriate: the early buildings in Oita, for example, demonstrated his preoccupation with space and the relationship between it and the participant and with highly formalized concrete structures. Both these architectural themes were followed through in his Gunma Museum of Modern Art of 1974 in which he combined a

Arata Isozaki, Okanoyama Graphic Art Museum 1982-3 Isozaki is one of Japan's most original architects, combining elements of Modernism – such as the use of glass blocks – with Post-Modern details, like the classical references and colours *(above right)*.

Arata Isozaki, Gunma Prefectural Museum of Fine Arts 1970–4 In this overtly Modern building, Isozaki stresses the strong aesthetic impact of the use of the grid which nevertheless has its roots in traditional Japanese architecture.

Arata Isozaki, Palladium Club 1980s This building again shows Isozaki's highly formal, subtle combination of the Modern and Post-Modern architectural languages.

Toyo Itoh, House in Nakano Honcho 1976 The move away from Metabolism in the early 1970s produced a number of architects, such as Itoh, who returned to traditional Japanese architecture in search of a 'purer' more minimal aesthetic for the domestic house.

traditional tea-room with a stunning Modernist-inspired grid structure in aluminium. Such is the technical perfection and high level of craftsmanship that Charles Jencks has claimed that Isozaki's work 'approaches the condition of modern jewellery'[3]. An important factor in his work is his interest in metaphysics, a definite departure from the overtly commercial work of so many Japanese architects in the 1960s.

The main tendency of Japanese architecture in the 1970s was to move away from the pro-consumerist attitudes of the Pop and early Post-Modern buildings towards a cooler, aestheticized 'Late-Modern' style. This was epitomized in the work of a large number of young architects, among them Kazuo Shinohara, Monta Mozuna, Mayumi Miyawaki, Hiroshi Hara and Toyo Itoh. This new sensibility was also characterized by a swing away from the urban ideal and a renewed interest in the poetics of space. It was a logical development given the lack of space which can be manipulated in the Japanese urban landscape. In his designs for private houses, Shinohara took up both these challenges and developed a highly minimal aesthetic which responded to both traditional Japanese architectural concepts and contemporary reality.

Japan of the late 1970s and early 1980s witnessed what has been described as a 'New Wave' in architecture. An exhibition with that very title, in fact, toured the USA in the late 1970s. There were signs in the architectural plans, photographs and drawings that comprised the exhibition that many of the young architects were grappling with the problems presented to them both by their traditional and their more immediate Modern heritages. The concept of Modernism, as formulated in Europe, still lingered in Japan as one of the major influences on contemporary architectural culture. The freedom to append to this Modernist base both indigenous traditional and Western references where appropriate was specific to the Japanese architectural movement and is one of its major strengths.

Typically, avant-garde activity and commercial reality fused in the work of the new Japanese designers, and buildings continued to be constructed on an ambitious scale. High-rise urban structures indicative of a flourishing capitalist economy – hotels, banks, and office buildings, many of which were designed by very large practices such as that of the Nikkon Sekkei group – continued to fill the urban Japanese skylines. A number of young architects meanwhile moved back to the very idiom which had inspired the early Modernists – the Japanese house. As Chris Fawcett has

Kazuo Shinohara, House in Uehara 1975
This house combines the subtlety of Shinohara's manipulation of internal space, his debt to Le Corbusier (in the inclusion of Thonet chairs), and his commitment to traditional Japanese architectural construction in the use of the beam.

Kazuo Shinohara, Cubic Forest House 1971 A domestic building, set in natural surroundings away from the urban conglomeration, this house looks back with reverence both to European Modernism and traditional Japanese aesthetic ideals.

explained 'a new resolve was set up by the Post-Metabolists to plumb Japan and its past to provide what might be a more exact model of what could be called distinctly Japanese. Concentrating on small, singular houses they found they could still enjoy the formal procedures embodied in the large-scale Metabolist projects but turned in more literary and ambiguous directions, affirming the architectural gesture as an idiosyncratic but necessary means of defining place'.[4]

Young architects, among them Yoji Watanabe, Itsuko Hasegawa and Kazuhiro Ishii, took on this particular challenge. Their central theme was to reject the inevitability of technological progress and the necessity for large-scale civic projects. Although still essentially oriented towards the city, these architects worked on a smaller scale, concentrating on private rather than public projects. In the late 1970s, Tadao Ando, for example, created a number of small-scale residences in which he attempted to find a resolution to many of the preoccupations of a number of his generation of architects. His response was to turn back to nature and make use of traditional Japanese sources, such as the wind and the environment. Although, like Isozaki, Ando was resistant to consumerism, several of his houses were built for leading members of the booming Japanese fashion industry. The patronage that this group could offer became an important aspect of much Japanese architecture

and interior design in the 1980s. Designs for store interiors, in particular (see chapter 7), demonstrate the way in which Japanese avant-garde ideas are integrated, through enlightened patronage, into everyday life. This contrasts with so many other countries in which the avant-garde remains on the periphery in a kind of utopian idealism.

Like so many of his precursors, Ando has integrated traditional Japanese features into his buildings. This is not a nostalgic gesture as he uses the traditional to enhance the stark Late-Modernism of his highly formalized structures. The use of reinforced concrete walls underlines his commitment to European Modernism, but the central emphasis is, in a traditional Japanese vein, on the interaction of his structures with their topographical setting, on their relationship with the wind, rain and other elements, and on their interplay with natural light. His architectural minimalism owes much to Le Corbusier as well as to traditional Japanese architecture. One project, the Rokko hillside housing project of 1983, clearly took its inspiration from Le Corbusier's Roq et Rob project for Cap Martin of 1946. The sparseness of Ando's structures, and of those of a number of his contemporaries, can be seen as a reaction to the confusion of modern Japanese cities. They are the result of striving for a visual order which had been lost in the decades of high consumerism, and a return to a form of spirituality.

Tadao Ando, Glass-Block Wall, Horiuchi Residence, Osaka 1979
This private house is composed of two blocks separated by an inner court. Ando has given careful thought to the different effects of the light penetrating the glass blocks at various times of the day.

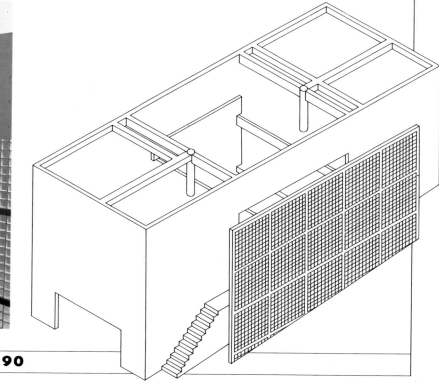

Tadao Ando, Rokko Housing 1983 Built on a steep southern slope overlooking a harbour, this collective housing project *(above)* is intended to be assimilated into nature. A yard is provided for the inhabitants' communal use.

Tadao Ando, Azuma House, Osaka 1976 One of the earliest of Ando's private residences, the Azuma House depends on the subtle manipulation of interior space that Ando was to exploit so effectively in the 1980s. A small court in the centre of the house makes the only contact with the exterior and the world of nature – in this case, light, air and rain.

Kisho Kurokawa, Wacoal Kojimachi Building, Tokyo 1984 These photographs are the exterior and interior views of the headquarters of a lingerie manufacturer. Kurokawa has moved beyond his earlier Metabolist phase into a new architectural idiom which combines Modern and Post-Modern interests with a commitment to traditional Japanese architectural aesthetics.

Kisho Kurokawa, Koshi Kaikan Centre, Toyama 1986 Built with stripes of aluminium threaded through it, this building is a centre for teachers and a hotel. It represents the architect's growing interest in the social role of architecture.

Kenzo Tange, Sogetsu Art Centre In this work, Tange embraces the purest form of international Modernism but, at the same time, retains an enormous debt to Buddhist-inspired traditional Japanese aesthetics. This is particularly evident in the interior *(left)*.

By the mid-1980s, two opposing strands have become visible within contemporary Japanese architecture. On the one hand, the Post-Modern movement, documented by Charles Jencks and evident in the numerous buildings in which symbolism, multivalence and eclecticism are all important, have become a familiar and highly integrated aspect of the Japanese architectural scene. At the same time, a much more austere, less compromising, purism has also emerged which in turn rejects the ornamentation associated with the Post-Modernist school of thought. In 1986, Ando wrote that 'to my eyes Post-Modernism appears to be just old wine in old bottles, with nostalgic ornamentation applied. I don't believe it provides a fundamental solution.'[5] He nevertheless sympathizes with the Post-Modernists' resistance to universalization but chooses a return to the natural as his way to strive against it. The divide in architecture is mirrored by the contrasting tendencies in Japanese industrial design and fashion in the 1980s – the former embracing all the overt signs of Post-Modernism, the latter reflecting the more minimalist approach.

The very contrast was, in itself, part a reflection of the schizophrenia, or pluralism, which resides at the heart of Japanese society. Charles Jencks has written that 'Japan, with its strong traditions of Buddhist pluralism sees nothing wrong with interweaving opposites. Their everyday life is based on accepting contradiction: Western dress and the kimono, Western social ideals and a traditional society'.[6] In the light of this analysis the essential contradictions within modern Japanese architecture – its incessant borrowings from the West and its search for an extension of its own indigenous traditions, its acceptance and rejection of symbolism and ornament – can be seen, not as a problem in need of a solution, but as a definite strength. Combined with the availability of patronage, this has given post-war Japanese architecture an advantage over its more univalent foreign equivalents.

The design of many of today's most interesting and innovative buildings comes from Japan, and Japanese architectural magazines are avidly scoured by aspiring architects the world over. Clearly the process of imitating foreign models combined with a determination to improve on them (by referring to the refined standards handed down by tradition) has served to put Japan well in front in architectural design.

Chapter 6

Graphics and packaging

*'Absorbing new materials and media and grafting them to
the traditional graphic heritage a successful national style has been produced
which is quite different to anything known in western graphic design'*[1]

The catalogue for the 1980 'Japan Style' exhibition held at the Victoria and Albert Museum in London pinpointed what it described as 'graphism' as being one of the central themes within both traditional and contemporary Japanese design. To illustrate this concept it selected a range of striking two-dimensional images from the surfaces of Japanese kites, ukiyo-e prints, playing cards, aprons worn by Sumo wrestlers and contemporary posters. They all manifested a rich graphic quality emphasizing flatness, linearity, bright colour and a special capacity for integrating imagery with typography. The same graphic tendency has been fundamental to Japanese design since 1945. As in architecture, Japan has evolved a striking modern graphic design movement largely as a result of combining indigenous traditions with its own version of Western Modernism.

Modern graphic art in the West owed much to the stimulus it received from Japan in the last decades of the nineteenth century. Japanese ukiyo-e prints first appeared in Europe from the 1860s onwards, used as the cheap wrapping around such imported goods as Japanese ceramics and lacquerwork; their impact upon the French poster artists of those years, among them Toulouse-Lautrec and Jules Cheret, was enormous and is well documented. The reciprocal involvement of Japanese poster designers with avant-garde European movements through the 1920s and 1930s has received less attention. Many young Japanese artists went to Germany and France to work with the practitioners of Constructivism and art deco and, in turn, took back much of what they had learned to Japan. Muneji Satomi, for example, a young Japanese designer who had worked in Paris through the 1930s produced, in 1937, a poster for the Japanese Government Railways which clearly owed a debt to the Cubist-inspired posters of Cassandre and others for the European transport authorities. Similarly,

posters were used commercially, along with advertisements and packaging in Japan between the wars, as they were in Europe; the work of Ayao Yamana and Mitsugu Maeda for the Shiseido cosmetics company was inspired, both conceptually and stylistically, by European, particularly French, models. For the most part, however, Japanese graphic design of the 1920s and 1930s lacked the intensity of the European movements and it was not until the post-war era that a Japanese Modern movement in graphic design emerged to rival those of Europe.

Nineteenth-century wood-block print
This print, depicting a horse-drawn tramway, is typical of the kind of cheap printed images that were produced for and bought by the newly wealthy Japanese middle-classes in the nineteenth century.

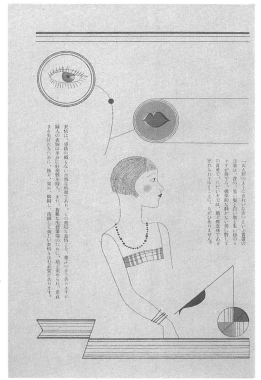

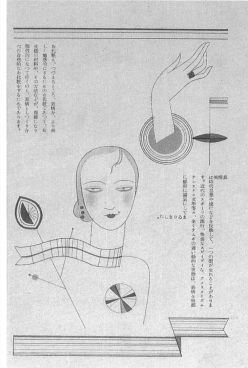

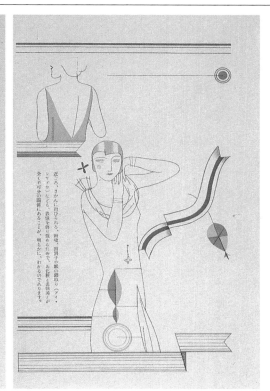

Ayao Yamana, Posters and fan for Shiseido 1930–2 Many Japanese graphic artists went to France in the 1920s and 1930s to work with the promoters of the art-deco style. This in turn had an enormous influence on pre-war Japanese graphics and, although much of the work lacked the intensity of the European models, a few examples, such as these posters for the Shiseido cosmetics company, were striking.

In the immediate post-war years paper and other materials associated with the graphic arts were in short supply. The most obvious influence of those years was American packaging, in evidence in Japan on the sweet and cigarette packets handed out by occupying troops, and soon Japanese packaging began to reflect the strongly commercial emphasis of American examples. Raymond Loewy's famous design for the 'Lucky Strike' cigarette pack became an icon of modern design for the newly emerging generation of young designers. Loewy was, in fact, approached in 1952 by the Japanese Monopoly Bureau – a body involved with the programme of manufacturing for reconstruction – to design a packet for a brand of Japanese cigarettes called 'Peace'. The simple stylized motif of a dove with a laurel leaf in its mouth which Loewy developed acted as a great stimulus to contemporary design and 'became the basis for the epoch of new design'.[2]

While the commercial world of American packaging provided one influence in post-war Japanese graphics, it was

Raymond Loewy, 'Peace' cigarette pack 1952 Raymond Loewy's design for the 'Peace' cigarette pack provided a model of graphic sophistication for Japanese packaging designers to emulate in the years following the Second World War.

paralleled by a more purist approach advocated by a number of designers and critics who were associated with the burgeoning 'Japanese Modern' movement. In this, the critic Masaru Katsumie played a vital role as the principal protagonist in a new graphic design movement which looked to European Constructivists such as Laszlo Moholy-Nagy for its inspiration. Born in 1909, Katsumie worked in

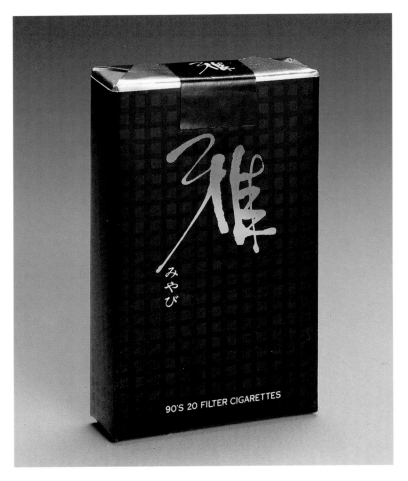

Kanome Takashi, 'Miyabi' cigarette pack This striking packet design for the Japan Cigarette Corporation owes its strong visual impact to the designer's clever use of Japanese calligraphy.

Kanome Takashi, 'Nori' pack Takashi's design for the 'Takara Kaiso' brand of Japanese dried seaweed draws heavily on traditional Japanese aesthetics in its use of simple, monochrome graphic imagery.

Kanome Takashi, 'Ryoku-cha' packs These highly original packaging designs are for the 'Mai Burendo' brand of green tea, manufactured by Fukujuen. The simple, uncluttered style is typically Japanese.

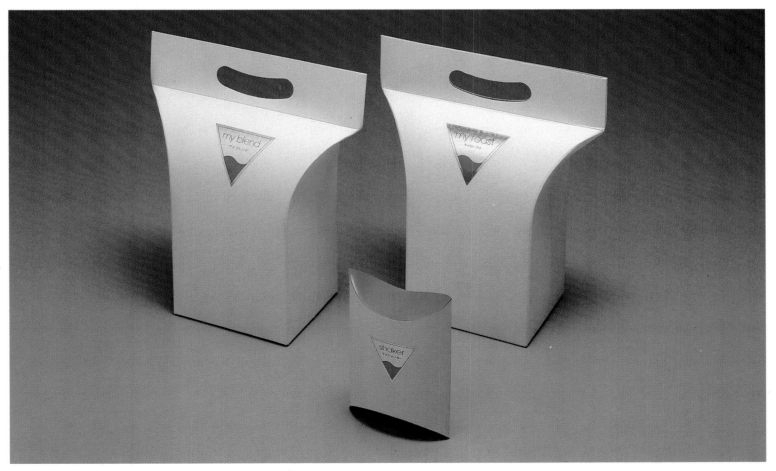

Yusaku Kamekura, Poster for Tokyo Olympic Games 1961 In contrast to the sophisticated technology of his later posters this simple image conveys its meaning through minimal graphic means.

Yusaku Kamekura, Poster for Tokyo Olympic Games 1962 Kamekura's striking poster for the 18th Olympic Games, held in 1964, shows the skilful way in which this Japanese graphic designer uses highly finished photographic images in his work.

the 1930s for the National Industry and Art Institute and in the 1940s he became a journalist on Japan's *Industrial Art News*. During this time he developed a particular interest in modern Japanese design, which continued through the 1940s and in to the 1950s when he was instrumental in helping to create a new Japanese design movement based on the European example. Katsumie's contributions included the organization of the 'Gropius and the Bauhaus' exhibition held at the National Museum of Modern Art in Tokyo in 1954; the formation, in the same year, of the Japanese Society for Science in Design (which stressed the role of rationalism in the modern design process, see chapter 2); and the publication in 1957 of a translation of Herbert Read's classic design text *Art and Industry*, and in 1958 of his own work *Good Design*.

In the 1950s it became clear that Japanese graphic designers were actively involved in organizing themselves professionally. In 1951, the Japan Advertising Artists' Club was formed in Osaka; in 1952 this was followed by the creation of the Tokyo Art Directors' Club; and in 1953 the first issue of *Idea* magazine was published. As a result of these stimuli and the number of designers involved, the Japanese graphic design profession became an effective and visible force. Many of the leading figures of the day – among them Takashi Kono, Yusaku Kamekura and Hiromu Hara – were associated with the Osaka-based movement of those years, working on posters, advertising and packaging for both the world of commerce and for countless Japanese cultural activities, including exhibitions and posters for ballets and plays. The ambitions of the group were clearly aligned with

Yusaku Kamekura, Pictograms for Tokyo Olympic Games 1964
One of the most significant contributions of Japanese graphic designers to international graphic design was this set of simple graphic signs which provided the basis for many similar schemes generated worldwide in subsequent years.

the Japanese 'good design' movement of the 1950s and Katsumie provided a bridge between the worlds of graphic and product design. In 1959 he launched the periodical *Graphic Design* in which he pursued a clear policy of promoting the European, in particular the Swiss, Constructivist aesthetic. The magazine quickly became the major mouthpiece for the Japanese profession. Katsumie later wrote that he had 'placed emphasis on the introduction of designers with a frankly constructivistic style' and claimed that 'rather than Raymond Savignac I selected Max Bill. Rather than Herbert Leupin I chose Joseph Muller-Brockmann.'[3]

The general ambition of the group was to free Japanese graphic design from its pre-war associations with 'applied art' and with its immediate post-war links with American commercialism, and to instil into it a more Modernist sensibility. As with architects, Constructivism was close to the hearts of Japanese designers on account of their traditional concept of space, their ideas about modularity, and their overtly ideogrammatic approach towards communication.

While a number of interesting posters, advertisements, and other pieces of graphic design were seen in Japan through the late 1950s, the rest of the world first became aware of these developments in the 1960s. The system of graphic signs evolved for the 1964 Olympic Games in Tokyo was highly instrumental in bringing Japanese ideas to international attention. The project was co-ordinated by Masaru Katsumie and consisted of a series of public information signs and pictograms depicting the various

Tadanori Yokoo, Poster 1966 More than any other post-war Japanese graphic designer Yokoo was responsible for moving the emphasis away from the high-minded ideals of Constructivism to the more mass culture-oriented, vibrant 'Pop' aesthetic which had an enormous impact on Japanese design in the 1960s and 1970s. This poster is entitled 'Koshimaki-Osen'.

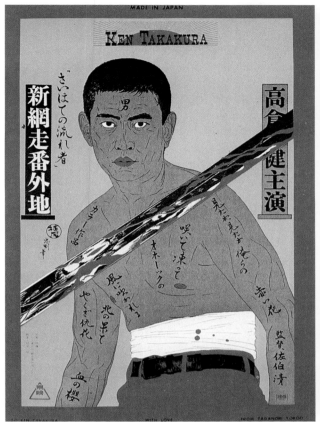

Tadanori Yokoo, Film poster 1969 Yokoo's interest in mass culture led him to design numerous, highly expressive film posters, like this one for the Toei studios' 'Ken Takakura', in the late 1960s.

Yusaku Kamekura, Poster for Expo '70 1967 Kamekura's proposal for a poster for Expo '70 demonstrates his continued interest in the idea of maximum communication through concise graphic means. His use of clean, geometric forms conveys his commitment to Modernism.

sporting activities. Its success encouraged the introduction of an international symbol system which was used for all the Olympic Games that came after the 1964 event. Katsumie went on to oversee the graphics for the 1970 World's Fair in Osaka and the 1972 Sapporo Winter Olympics in a similar manner.

The 1964 Olympics scheme represented the high point of the rationally based graphics movement of the post-war era. This movement also reached its apogee in the work of graphic designers Yusaku Kamekura, who was responsible for the design for the Olympic pictograms of 1964, and in that of Mitsuo Katsui, who adhered more faithfully to the ideas of the European Modern design movement. Katsui employed the principle of 'basic design' – that is, assembling an image through a modular, constructional process – inherited from the German, Dutch and Swiss schools of Modernist graphic design. Like many of his contemporaries he used the most advanced forms of print technology available and evolved a very tight graphic style. His work on the Kodansha encyclopedia was pioneering in the field of book design and his 'Zen-on Music Calendar' is in the design collection of the Museum of Modern Art in New York.

In sharp contrast to that of Katsui, the work of Tadanori Yokoo in the mid-1960s was inspired by a much more 'Pop'-oriented sensibility and he led a movement which used bright colours and a much freer approach than that of the more mainstream Constructivists. Linked more closely to fine art Yokoo's work rejected the highly rational approach of the previous decade. In the early 1980s his work became increasingly expressionistic and painterly and he proclaimed himself no longer a graphic designer but a fine artist. 'I believe design will move in the direction of useless design,'[4] he wrote. For him, the term 'useless' in design means not primarily functional, but having an expressive poetic quality – a prediction which with the emergence of a highly expressive graphics movement in the early 1980s started to become a reality.

The late 1960s and 1970s witnessed a particularly inventive and diverse era in Japanese graphic design. The pioneering generation – including such individuals as Ikko Tanaka, Shigeo Fukuda and Kiyoshi Awazu, as well as those already mentioned – continued to produce subtle and sophisticated advertisements and posters which impressed the Western world and won international prizes. In 1977 J. J. de Lucio-Meyer wrote that 'the importance of the eastern creative mind is apparent to everyone searching into the very basic techniques of graphics as we know them today'.[5] American air-brushing techniques, as used by Harumi Yamaguchi for an image of a girl in baseball gear in an advertisement for Manns' wines, sat alongside much more traditional indigenous subject matter in the work of Awazu and Keisuke Nagamoto, which in turn paralleled the striking photographic poster work of Gan Hosoya and the sketchy linear simplicity of Shigeo Fukuda's 'Friendship' and 'Accident' posters. All these pieces – whether produced for commercial, social or cultural patrons – were characterized by their technical excellence and a display of confidence. The maturity that this demonstrated had been achieved, essentially, by a fusion of high technology, a firm grounding in Modern European ideals and a continued awareness of the role of traditional Japanese culture. The sophistication of Japanese graphic design and its difference from Western counterparts, is the result of this unique fusion of elements. Throughout the late 1960s and 1970s companies such as Sony and Suntory took advantage of the new inventiveness, producing ranges of highly sophisticated advertising material in these years. The department stores also acted as very important patrons of the new graphic design movement, many of them employing their own in-house art departments to produce display work, and advertising.

Advertisement for Suntory whisky 1979 The technological sophistication of this whisky advertisement is matched by the subtlety of its message. Linked by a common culture, Japanese society is able to understand the meaning of graphic images which a Western audience would find obscure and incomprehensible.

Advertisement for Sony Walkman 1979 The Sony Corporation took advantage of Japanese graphic designers' skill in producing highly effective, technically sophisticated images. This photograph for an advertisement for the first Walkman is a prime example.

Kiyoshi Awazu, Poster 1980 Awazu was among the pioneering avant-garde of Japan's post-war graphic artists. This striking poster was designed to publicize a print exhibition at the Art Front Gallery in Tokyo.

One specific area in which traditional concepts continued to dominate in the post-war years was packaging. More than any other people, the Japanese had developed a culture of the package, to the extent that different regions evolved their own distinct forms for small consumer goods, among them sweets, cakes, bottles of sake and tablets of soap. A traditional 'bento-baku' (lunch box), 'kyogi' (box made of thin wood), and 'furoshiki' (piece of square cloth for wrapping) had all been in use for many years, and paper, straw, bamboo sheaths and leaves were all commonly used for packing – the latter two in the well-known bundle of five eggs (an archetypal package design) and in the 'chimaki' (wrapped rice dumplings).

A great sense of respect for these refined traditions has prevailed in the work of Japan's best-known designers of packaging – among them Katsu Kimura and Kanome Takashi. Kimura raised packaging beyond its mere commercial application to an art form, evolving, through the 1960s and 1970s, a range of original packages which went far beyond the simple requirements of function. In his 'Box and Cox' exhibition of 1979 he presented a range of cubic modules of fruit, which peeled open in imitation of the fruits they represented. In his more commercial work Kimura has developed styles which are appropriate to the product in question, such as the use of calligraphy in packages for traditional sweets (candies).

Eiko Ishioka, Motoko Naruse and Kyoko Inui, Poster 1979
Photographed by Kazumi Kurigami, this poster produced for a media campaign shows how Japanese graphic designers use high-class photography to stunning effect. A surrealistic mood pervades this image which is entitled 'Can East Wear West?'.

Katsu Kimura, Packaging designs
Kimura uses simple, striking graphic motifs carefully combined with lettering in his highly original designs for packaging. The series for 'Cafe sta' instant coffee was produced in 1984. The packaging *(above)* is a 1979 design for 'Kokkoan' (Japanese cakes).

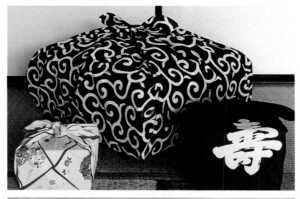

'Furoshiki'
Traditional packaging continues to inspire contemporary practice of this art. These examples of the traditional knotted package, or 'furoshiki', are in silk and cotton.

'Meigaramai bento'
The traditional compartmentalized lunch box expertly conveys the Japanese talent for skilful packaging which continues today.

FRANCIS COPPOLA'S FILM "APOCALYPSE NOW"

地 獄 の 黙 示 録

戦争は魅力的だ。そこには美と魅力があるに違いない。さもなければ人類はこんなにも始終戦争を繰り返しているはずはない。——フランシス・コッポラ

Eiko Ishioka, Motoko Naruse and Kyoko Inui, Film poster 1979 Illustrated in 'hyper-real' style by Haruo Takino, and designed by a team of graphic artists, this poster for 'Apocalypse Now' successfully evokes the atmosphere of the film.

Inevitably, at the mass market end of the spectrum, the use of plastics began to dominate that of paper and wood by the late 1960s. At the same time, American models influenced many of the cartons, bottles, tins and packets that poured into the Japanese market-place. It seemed that the days of the traditional package were numbered. The oil crisis of 1973 reversed the trend, to a certain extent, and encouraged a move in many quarters back to a consideration of traditional materials and techniques.

The most striking graphic manifestation of Japan in the 1980s has been the sense of growing disillusionment with the wonders of high technology, and with the impeccable finish which could be achieved through high-class printing. This has prompted a retreat back from high-gloss photographic reproduction to a looser, more sketchy and 'unfinished' aesthetic. The new illustrators of the 1980s –

among them Katsuhiko Hibino, Emiko Shimoda, Keiji Ito and Makoto Nakamura – whose work has crowded the pages of the ever expanding numbers of magazines and the surfaces of the growing piles of advertising material, favours a rough, sketchy style which reasserts the expressive role of the individual and the use of the hand. The work of Tadanori Yokoo has been highly influential and has promoted a fine-art consciousness in a new generation of graphic designers to the extent that a writer in *Graphic Design* magazine commented, in March 1985, that 'the first half of the 1980s was a time of the waves of newcomers which are said to come only once in ten years'.[6]

One of the more prominent areas where this 'new wave' was being felt was in record cover design. Part of the expanding and innovative youth movement of the 1980s, the medium lent itself to inventiveness and expression. The

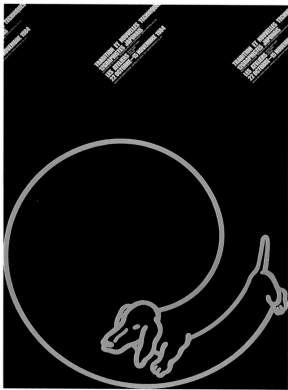

Shigeo Fukuda, Poster 1984 This design is typical of Fukuda, who has played a major role in post-war Japanese graphics. Based on a simple yet sophisticated image, it was produced to publicize an exhibition of Japanese graphic design held in Paris.

Makoto Nakamura, Exhibition poster 1984 This striking poster, based on a photographic image, was designed for the same exhibition of graphic design.

Eiko Ishioka, Production design 1984 In addition to the film posters, Ishioka also works directly with film sets, costumes, and props. This scene is from the film 'Mishima'.

Close-up of Japan London 1985

SEIJI OZAWA conducting THE NEW JAPAN PHILHARMONIC
JAPAN NEW MUSIC FORUM
ISSEY MIYAKE : BODYWORKS—Fashion Without Taboos
TADASHI SUZUKI and SCOT(Waseda Sho-Gekijo): The Trojan Women

MITSUI GROUP

**Ikko Tanaka, Poster
1985** In contrast to the
high-gloss photographic
images that proliferated
in the 1970s, Tanaka, as
this colourful poster for
a festival of Japanese
cultural events held in
London in 1985 shows,
continued to
demonstrate his
commitment to the
Constructivist tradition
of graphic design.

Koijo Ito, Magazine advertisement 1986 This advertisement for a computer school demonstrates the 'new wave' in contemporary Japanese graphic design. Ito has rejected the high-technology 'good taste' look, replacing it with a use of 'primitive' illustrated images.

work of Koichi Hara, for example, showed just how close to fine art graphic design could be. One singular tendency in record cover design of the early 1980s was the introduction of a minimal aesthetic and the use of monotones. This represented a rejection of both the complexity of image and the bright colours associated with the 'Pop'-inspired work of the 1960s, and of the slick, high-gloss designs of the 1970s. The 'reduction to essentials' principle indicated a return from the 'anything is possible' route implied by high technology. An absence of typography in these designs aligned them with what has been described as the 'no label

quality goods' style which applauds the elimination of unnecessary decoration and the use of bare form. A technique much loved by the designers of fashion boutiques as well in these years, and by contemporary architects, it clearly owed much to traditional Japanese aesthetic values.

Today contemporary Japanese graphic designers remain energetic and open to ideas from every direction. They are also ready to incorporate these ideas into forms which take into account indigenous traditions, from both the distant and the immediate past. This pluralist approach makes current graphics one of the most exciting areas of design in Japan.

Chapter 7

Fashion

*'The Japanese clothes have a basic kind of comfort
that allows me to feel like a human being,
not a captive of my clothes.'*[1]

The story of Japanese fashion design is both brief and extraordinary. As in so many other design fields, Japan's successes in the world of fashion derive from the tensions that exist between Western inspiration and the perpetuation of traditional Japanese values. From this opposition has emerged a brand new formula which has captivated the rest of the world to the extent that, in the 1980s, the Japanese are actually pointing the way forward to countries such as France and Italy – the long-standing leaders in this field. This is quite remarkable, given that the Japanese have only really adopted Western dress (despite earlier flirtations) and the Western concept of clothing-as-fashion since 1945. Today the kimono, and other traditional garments, which have always been 'pure' items of clothing, are worn only by the old, and in some rural areas; and it is difficult to remember that the kimono was the norm before the Second World War.

Along with shipbuilding, the textile industry led the Japanese industrial developments of the last years of the nineteenth century. This strength permitted Japan to move quickly into the production of fashion garments, at first just for the domestic market but later also for export. It has developed steadily in the years since 1945 to the extent that Japan now has a thriving fashion industry: leading manufacturers such as Nicole and Pink House cater for a mass market both at home and abroad.

Although a system of fashion education was instigated in Tokyo in the 1950s, with the foundation of the Bunka College (where the most noted professor was Chie Koike), many young Japanese designers have gone to Europe, in particular to Paris, to learn at the feet of the acknowledged masters of *haute couture*. Unlike architecture and graphic design, however, where many practitioners have gained international renown since 1945, the reputation of post-war Japanese fashion design is founded on only a few names.

The first Japanese fashion designer to make a mark was Hanae Mori. She opened a studio in Tokyo in the 1950s to design costumes for films, and soon developed a number of private clients as well, going on to open a couture house. The model she emulated was the one established by the Parisian *haute couture* industry and in the 1960s she spent time in Paris learning at first hand how the system operated. She took her experience back to Japan where she now owns and runs a number of large-scale companies – among them Studio V – producing wholesale fashion items aimed at the youth market.

Mori has indeed become a legend in her own lifetime and her influence on a generation of younger Japanese fashion designers has been considerable. Nevertheless, her designs are largely Western in style and inspiration, although they are tempered by the inclusion of small Japanese details which have given them a particular flavour.

The principal contribution of Japanese fashion to the West and the reason for its enormous popularity, has been its creation of a new image of the modern woman. Kenzo Takada has been much more overtly Japanese in inspiration, and was the next Japanese designer to make an impact on the West, the first to offer an alternative to the Parisian example of *haute couture*. He went to Paris at the age of twenty-five and worked there through the 1960s, selling designs to, among others, Louis Féraud, but did not launch his own collection of factory-made clothes, under the 'Jap' label, until 1970. That same year, he opened a boutique of the same name in Paris. His highly original designs were soon in demand. Kenzo rejected the 'over-perfection' of high fashion and attempted to evolve a new philosophy for women's clothing, which was based essentially on geometry, and emphasized the use of natural fabrics. Kenzo, and others who have followed him, has developed a clothing idiom which

Kenzo, prêt-à-porter 1983 Kenzo was one of the first Japanese fashion designers to make an impact in the West. In the early 1970s he was known for the way he combined the loose cut and natural fabrics of traditional Japanese clothing with the bright colours of 'Pop'.

Kenzo, prêt-à-porter 1983 The loose, untailored cut and the use of crisp natural cotton in this design are features which have characterized Kenzo's work for two decades.

derives from the kimono in that it creates space between the body and the cloth, rather than custom-making clothing to fit individuals. This is in sharp contrast to Western fashion, which has long been characterized by an emphasis on female sexuality expressed by tailored clothing which fits the body and emphasizes its shape. Kenzo's image has contributed to the decline of *haute couture* as Paris had defined it and prompted a move towards a more standardized, democratic notion of fashion.

Kenzo is said to have taken many of his designs from architecture, in particular from the buildings of his home, Himeji on Honshu, and a sense of the geometrical construction of natural fabrics pervaded much of his work in the early 1970s. This was emphasized by his use of such devices as quilting and padding to encourage fabrics to stand away from the body in the manner of much traditional Japanese clothing. The 1971 Jap collection, consisting of a number of items all made from fine white cotton, exemplified this approach perfectly. One long white dress featured a tucked bodice, puffed and cuffed sleeves, and a quilted bib. It hung loosely on the model who was photographed alongside a man in the karate outfit which had clearly inspired many of its details.

Kenzo's collections have combined Western and Eastern ideas, and he was clearly influenced, as were many other Japanese designers in various fields, by the Pop movement

Kenzo, prêt-à-porter 1984 The bright colours of Kenzo's fashion clothing of the 1980s echo his earlier designs which were influenced by the Pop culture of the 1960s – a formative decade in Kenzo's career.

of the 1960s. In fashion, 'Pop' was seminal in facilitating the departure from *haute couture* and allowing fashion to become both ready-made and young in inspiration. In the early 1970s Kenzo presented a collection consisting of a set of brightly coloured, schoolgirl-inspired tunics, ties, socks and berets with many of the fabrics embellished by checks and stripes. By the middle of the decade he had evolved a style which emphasized voluminous, loose-fitting clothing in natural fabrics like cotton, drill, poplin, raw silk and linen, executed both in very vibrant and in more neutral colours (black, white and khaki). His clothes became highly desirable and widely emulated and they sold well in Paris, London and New York.

The strongly 'architectural' style of Kenzo Takada is in sharp contrast to the work of Kansai Yamamoto, another young Japanese fashion designer who began to make a strong impact in Europe in the early 1970s. He provided a striking image of decorative exoticism which has its roots in the dramatic traditions of Japanese kabuki theatre. Stuck-on, ready-made imagery owing much to Pop painting, displaying such motifs as a *samurai* in satin, are appliquéd on to the surfaces of large T-shirts, and loose-fitting dresses and coats. One satin coat from 1971 was covered with navy and white cotton discs filled with butterflies while another had a satin figure committing *hara-kiri* applied to its back. Like Kenzo, Kansai often uses simple black cotton but his

Yohji Yamamoto, Summer collection 1982 In sharp contrast to Kenzo's vibrant tones, Yamamoto, along with Rei Kawakubo, reverted to the simplicity of black, white and grey in his 'unstructured' designs of the 1980s.

Issey Miyake, Summer collection 1982 In his dramatic designs for women's clothing Miyake went further than anyone else in the 1970s in bringing 'East' to meet 'West'.

Issey Miyake, Spring/ Summer collection 1983 The hallmark of Miyake's designs is his use of layer upon layer of voluminous natural fabrics in muted tones.

garments are embellished in a far more dramatic and graphic way. His references to Japanese culture were at this time much more overt; his models had wooden combs in their hair and were made up in the traditional kabuki manner. Today, Kansai's work retains that same combination of Japanese decorative, graphic sumptuousness and Western Pop culture and it has earned itself a special place in the contemporary fashion market.

The seeds of the modern Japanese fashion design movement were largely sown, therefore, in the 1970s with the work of Japanese designers who were based in Europe and were influenced by the styles of the mid and late sixties. Michiko, for instance, claims that the 1960s were the inspiration behind her padded coats and peasanty jackets.

Building on the break-throughs of the 1970s Japanese fashion has taken off internationally in the 1980s. A seminal figure of this advance has been Issey Miyake. More than anybody else he has established the anti-structural, anti-perfect look as a real alternative to tailored fashion. He went straight from the Tama University in Tokyo to Paris in 1965 to study at the Chambre Syndicale de la Couture Parisienne. The following year he worked as an assistant to Guy Laroche and from there he went on, in 1968, to work with another Parisian master, Hubert de Givenchy. Miyake says that the experience of being in Paris during the student riots of 1968 was a formative one for him, in that the mood of liberation helped him to abandon finally the shackles of Parisian *haute couture* and its high cultural overtones. He has written that 'the posed formality of *haute couture* seemed antipathetic'[2] and while he clearly absorbed the approach to fashion that surrounded him in Paris in the 1960s he was ready, by 1970, to reject it all and 'to start again at the beginning by peeling away all the layers'.[3] After a couple of years spent in New York working with Geoffrey Beene on his ready-to-wear collections, Miyake returned to Tokyo in 1970 and began working in a way which brought together his Western experience and his knowledge of traditional Japanese fabrics and clothing.

While his early creations were quite clearly Pop-inspired, like Kenzo before him Miyake made use of cottons and quilting and, in the early 1970s went on to produce, a range of clothes which consisted, essentially, of pieces of irregularly shaped fabric which hung loosely around the body. He then built up the fabric in layers, draping and wrapping it as a means of creating volume and form. The main emphasis was on texture – achieved through the use of wrinkles, pleats and smocking – and his clothes began to take on a sculptural quality which has remained Miyake's

Issey Miyake, Spring/ Summer collection 1984 The loose forms of this highly 'classical' outfit allow the drapes of the cloth to create their own space.

Issey Miyake, Autumn/Winter collection 1983–4 The untailored forms of Miyake's fashion designs recall traditional Japanese clothing in which there is always a space between the body and the garment.

Issey Miyake, Bodyworks In this cage-like bodice Miyake eroded the distinction between clothing and sculpture thereby giving fashion design a whole new dimension.

Issey Miyake, Spring/ Summer collection 1987 Miyake continues to design loose-fitting, casual clothing in a style that is all his own. By the 1980s he had multiplied the number of his international outlets, and now caters for a wide sector of the market.

trademark to the present day. He has explained that 'I like to work in the spirit of the kimono. Between the body and the fabric there exists only an approximate contact'.[4]

Through the 1970s Miyake retained a strong sense of theatre in the presentation of his clothes. In 1976, for instance, he presented 'Issey Miyake and Twelve Black Girls', and in 1977 'Fly with Issey Miyake', a spectacular show. Inevitably, with all the detailed work and vast quantities of fabric involved in each item the price of his creations remained high and his clientèle fairly exclusive. In 1980, however, the year in which he created the costumes for Maurice Béjart's ballet *Casta Diva*, he branched out into a number of subsidiary companies – including Issey Sport and

Plantation – which brought his designs to a wider market.

However exclusive and allied with fine art many of his pieces have remained, the philosophy behind Miyake's approach to design has been essentially democratic. He sees clothes as 'tools for living'[5]; they should be relaxing, convenient and useful and these principles have inspired his ready-to-wear clothing as well. His designs for private clients have, inevitably, been more exotic in nature: his 'Winged Victory', for instance, from his first Paris show of 1973, consisted of 15 square metres of material. All his clothing designs suggest a natural freedom, expressed through the simplicity of their cut, the abundance of materials, the space between the garment and the body, and

Issey Miyake, Spring/ Summer collection 1987 In his 1987 collection Miyake's sculptural approach has inspired garments which are, nonetheless, eminently wearable.

their general flexibility. Miyake has succeeded, on the one hand, in turning the kimono into an item of liberation and, on the other, in proposing radical clothing concepts which challenge the conventional meanings of dress. An exhibition he created in 1983, 'Bodyworks', which was seen in Japan, the USA and England, presented his clothes philosophy. Halfway between sculpture and clothing, the exhibition contained black silicon mannequins dressed in neoprene wetsuits, paper raincoats and rattan cages. For Miyake, as body sculptor, no material was exempt from use, be it 'iron, paper, cane, bamboo or stones'.[6] He has helped to take clothing into a new category of 'anti-fashion' by both leading it into a world of fine art where texture and volume are all-important, and by emphasizing comfort and freedom rather than 'sexiness' and 'fashion'.

The new wave of young Japanese designers who came to international prominence in the early 1980s followed Miyake's direction, aggressively asserting the same 'anti-fashionable' approach and promoting clothing in quite a new way. While the 1970s' designers had flourished on the basis of the tension created by their recognition of the values of both West and East, the 1980s' generation, whose best-known practitioners were Rei Kawakubo and Yohji Yamamoto, were much more openly Japanese in their commitments and affiliations. Ironically, they quickly became huge international successes and had, by the

**Rei Kawakubo,
Autumn/winter
collection 1986/7**
With its dramatically
asymmetrical detail,
Kawakubo's design for
her 'Comme des
Garçons' collection
demonstrates her debt to
the concept of
'imperfection' which
derives from traditional
Japanese aesthetics.

mid-1980s, established a radical new movement in the world of contemporary fashion design.

In contrast to Kenzo who had subtly introduced Japanese details into his otherwise predominantly Western designs, Rei Kawakubo, the founder of the Comme des Garçons range of shops, and Yohji Yamamoto have been much more aggressive in their determination to introduce 'Japaneseness' into their work. Kawakubo took part in the Paris collections for the first time in 1981 although she had opened a shop in Tokyo eight years before. Her designs were founded on a belief that Western contemporary fashion did not work for today's working women. She therefore proposed a range of clothes which would 'fulfil the same function for women that men's clothes have for years performed for men'.

Graduates of Keio University (Kawakubo has a degree in philosophy and no formal design training), both Kawakubo and Yamamoto base their design work on a firm belief that women should no longer be seen as sex objects but as working members of the community. What began as a strictly functional definition of clothing has become,

however, a high fashion movement in which clothes no longer need to look neat, tidy or glamorous and in which colour and other signs of 'obvious attractiveness' are mostly absent. Both of them now also work on designs for men's clothing. Again, they base these styles on the kimono – the garments are loose fitting, and untailored, intended to reduce or eliminate any element of 'sexuality'.

Like her predecessors, Kawakubo emphasizes the use of materials and inventive cutting. She also uses only natural dyes – among them calligrapher's sumi ink for her grey pieces. She dries silks and natural rayons in the sun to create a crinkled effect and, above all, follows the traditional Japanese concept of imperfection or 'sabi' in the use of outside seams, irregular proportions and asymmetrical hemlines. As a fashion style her work has had international impact and has been widely emulated. While overseas her garments are quite expensive and exclusive, in Japan the prices are competitive and they are bought by a young, fashion-conscious market.

In addition to their strong, uncompromising ideas on clothing, Kawakubo and her contemporaries have also pioneered a new approach towards the packaging and selling of their clothes – an approach which, in concept although not in style, stemmed from the European retail revolution of the 1960s. The fashion boutique, which had developed in London in the 'swinging sixties' through the work of such pioneers as Mary Quant and John Stephen became, in the 1980s, in Tokyo and elsewhere a highly sophisticated concept integral to the new movement in Japanese fashion. While the boutique of the 1960s was highly decorated and visually cluttered, its eighties equivalent is, in sharp contrast, uncompromising and monochrome. As such it provides a stark yet striking stage setting for the display of a handful of fairly shapeless clothes which are arranged in colour groupings – black, white and grey, with perhaps a hint of colour to suggest a contrast.

The American Comme des Garçons' interiors – among the most dramatic executed – were designed by the Japanese architect Takao Kawasaki. These highly aestheticized environments are characterized by large areas of blank concrete relieved only by the inclusion of a couple of black leather and chrome chairs chosen to emphasize the stark 'Modernism' of the concept. The chairs function as stones in

Takao Kawasaki, Comme des Garçons Tricot, Tokyo 1982
The stark interior of Kawakubo's knitwear store, conceived by her and developed by Kawasaki, demonstrates the way she has combined the idea of minimalism, associated with traditional Japanese aesthetics, with the 'brutalism' of bare concrete, inherited from the European Modern Movement. Goods become 'art' in this gallery-like setting.

Studio 80, Interior for Seiseian store, Tokyo 1986 The brightly coloured, co-ordinated fashion items displayed here look all the more vivid against the backdrop of the store's sober interior scheme.

Comme des Garçons store interior, New York The site in New York's 'SoHo' area provided Kawakubo with one of her most dramatic settings. The starkness of the concrete is relieved only by a few items of Modern Movement furniture.

Hanae Mori, Spring/ Summer collection 1987 The pioneer of Modern Japanese fashion design, Mori remains one of the country's leading figures in this area although, as this printed chiffon dress shows, her designs are both more conservative and more Westernized than those of the younger designers.

Michiko collection Michiko's innovative designs for the youth market made an impact in Britain in the early 1970s and were instrumental in bringing to the West an awareness of the new fashion talent emerging from the East.

a Zen Buddhist garden: they help to empty the mind in order that it can begin to fill again. They also show the lingering importance of the ethic and aesthetic of Modernism in Japanese design of the 1980s. In line with the new minimalist Japanese domestic architectural movement the new fashion boutiques depend on age-old Japanese aesthetic concepts, translated into the highly commercial world of international fashion. The Tokyo branch of Comme des Garçons, situated in the Axis building, the city's design altar, is the most extreme of all Kawakubo's environments – all the clothes are concealed behind two screens of opaque etched glass.

By the mid-1980s the Japanese fashion movement was thriving, with younger designers – among them Yoshiki Hishimima, who worked with Miyake before turning freelance – rising to prominence, and beginning to market their skills successfully. Like the new wave of young architects, Hishimima looks to natural forces like light and the wind, rather than to the urban landscape, as a source of inspiration. In so doing, he once again blurs the boundary between clothing, sculpture and traditional Japanese culture. In 1981, for example, he used 5,000 metres of bright pink fabric to make a design in the shape of a flower.

The new Japanese fashion movement which burst on to the world scene in the early 1980s was widely emulated. The main reason for this would appear to be that current Japanese fashion designs provide a valid alternative to mainstream *haute couture* for both sexes. Not only have the loose untailored styles produced by such people as Issey Miyake, Rei Kawakubo and Yohji Yamamoto, found a ready market among those who find the tailored look outdated and restricting, but their emphasis on natural fabrics and dyes, in place of man-made fibres, has proved in tune with thinking in the 1980s. The 'imperfect' look which results from this combination of elements has proved highly popular and shows no signs of diminishing in appeal.

Chapter 8

Furniture

Ironically, for a country in which furniture has only a limited traditional base, furniture design in Japan has become one of the most fertile contemporary design areas.

The traditional Japanese house contains only a minimal amount of storage furniture and the bare necessities for performing such activities as eating and writing from a sitting position on the floor. Western-style furniture and interior design were only introduced into Japan in the late-nineteenth century, and were then used primarily by the wealthy and fashionable for formal occasions and in public spaces. When Frank Lloyd Wright designed his Imperial Hotel, he found a huge gulf between Eastern and Western styles in interiors – a problem he solved by reducing the amount of furniture to a minimum.

After the Second World War the presence of American troops in Japan created a new demand for Western-style furniture and a number of designers found employment in this expanding sector. The Japanese furniture industry was under-developed and craft-based, but it responded to the demands of the time. The industry expanded in the post-war period as the Western life-style became increasingly common in Japan, and furniture was soon to be found commonly at first in public and commercial spaces, then in the home as well.

Early post-war attempts at furniture design were strongly influenced by the current international fashion for Scandinavian domestic style. Its particular appeal to the Japanese sensibility derived from its dependence on traditional materials, including wood and cane. A strong Scandinavian emphasis on craftsmanship also blended well with the traditional Japanese approach to design. A number of leading Japanese designers of the day – among them Sori Yanagi, Riki Watanabe and Isamu Kenmochi – soon created items of furniture which, although clearly Western in inspiration, were not inappropriate to their own traditions. Yanagi's 'Butterfly' stool of 1959, for example, combined a respect for traditional materials with sculptural form inspired by the curves on the roof of a Buddhist temple.

Continuous efforts were made, through the 1950s, 1960s and 1970s, to develop a specifically Japanese style in modern furniture. The most successful items attempted to incorporate traditional features of Japanese culture, such as sitting on the floor – as in Kenji Fujimori's dining set of 1966 for the Tendo Company – or the use of hand-made paper in lighting – as in Isamu Noguchi's famous 'Akari' light produced by the Yamigawa Company. On the whole, however, the vast majority of mass-produced furniture was either imported into Japan from the West or designed along Western lines.

By the 1980s, there were signs that a new, avant-garde Japanese furniture movement which brought together early and late twentieth-century Western preoccupations with a distinctly Japanese approach was emerging. Japanese furniture design and construction – of chairs, in particular – derive from the impact of Modernism and, subsequently, of Post-Modernism. In the Modernist school of thought, furniture design is inextricably linked with architecture, and it has become a major form of cultural expression in the years since 1900 in those countries which have a long-standing furniture-making tradition. It is that Modern tradition, rather than any traditional indigenous values, that has inspired the work in furniture design that has emerged from Japan in the 1980s. Given the importance of Japan's impact on the evolution of European Modernism, it is not inappropriate that both Modernist and Post-Modernist ideas should be re-imported into Japan, even if through the somewhat unfamiliar medium of furniture. It is also a strong symbol of the country's growing internationalism through this century and a mark of its growing enthusiasm for, and adoption of, Western-style living patterns.

Two of Japan's leading contemporary furniture designers are Shiro Kuramata and Shigeru Uchida. Both men straddle the Modernist/Post-Modernist schools but are also highly conscious of their country's traditional design values in their work. Kuramata was trained in woodwork and moved into display work, then interior and industrial design before

Shiro Kuramata, 'Imperial' cabinets 1981 Along with Masanori Umeda, Kuramata was one of the Japanese designers who contributed to the Memphis furniture collection in Milan which first shocked the design world in 1981. His Imperial cabinets are much more elegant and restrained than many of the flamboyant objects shown there.

Shiro Kuramata, 'Drawers in irregular forms' 1970 Kuramata's range of shaped chests with many drawers take furniture away from the world of mere utility into that of sculpture. They exert a strong presence on the space around them, functioning both as monoliths and as storage units.

Shiro Kuramata, 'Ritz' 1981 Kuramata's painted wooden chair design for the first Memphis collection in Milan, in spite of its unconventional design, is highly elegant. It retains a sense of Japanese grace in its proportions.

settling on furniture in the early 1970s. His furniture designs, among them chests in unorthodox shapes with numerous small drawers built into them, and chairs, are dependent on a minimalist aesthetic and concept of proportion which derive from traditional Japanese architecture and storage furniture. Their visual strength lies in their strong compositional values.

Kuramata's closeness to the West was demonstrated by his involvement with the Milan-based Memphis group from 1981 to 1983. Headed by Ettore Sottsass, Memphis produced

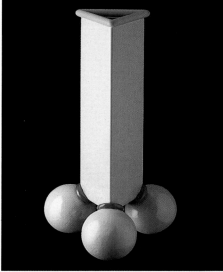

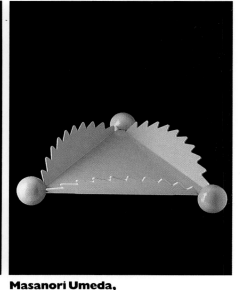

Masanori Umeda, 'Orinoco' 1983 Many contemporary Japanese architects/furniture designers have extended their interests beyond furniture to domestic objects executed in other media. This ceramic vase, designed for the third Memphis show, shows how Umeda injects humour into what is in Japan a revered art form.

Masanori Umeda, 'Parana' 1983 Another ceramic design from the third Memphis collection, this piece demonstrates how Umeda has exchanged the traditional craft aesthetic for a more Pop-inspired idiom.

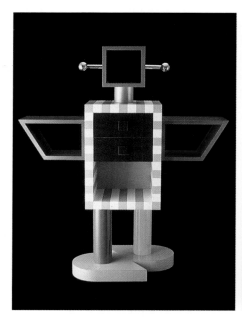

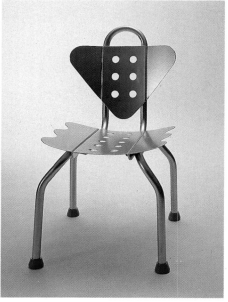

Masanori Umeda, 'Ginza' 1982 In the spirit of 'Post-Modernism', Umeda's robot cabinet, exhibited at the second Memphis show in Milan, functions more as an image than as a craft object.

Masanori Umeda, Aluminium chair 1985 Umeda's latest chair designs show the architect's continued commitment to expressive form and the importance for him of furniture as a vehicle of communication.

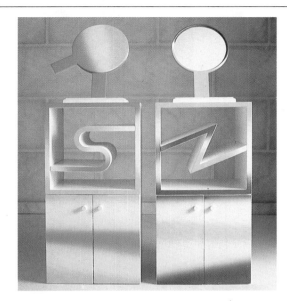

Arata Isozaki, 'Fuji' 1981 Isozaki's humorous little dressing table units were exhibited at the first Memphis show. They are one of the architect's few forays into furniture design.

Post-Modern experimental furniture, glass and ceramics. Kuramata's work for them included, in the first year, 'Ritz', a small writing desk in green-painted wood, and 'Imperial' cabinets, which were characterized by a distinctly Japanese sense of elegance and rectilinearity. His set of drawers of 1982, mounted on a tall metal base, was noticeably more serene than the other, more zany Memphis items, while in 1983 he ventured into vivid decoration with some stunning experiments in terrazzo on the surfaces of his small coffee table.

Two other Japanese designers, the architect Arata Isozaki and Masanori Umeda, also contributed items to the Memphis group exhibitions. In 1981, Isozaki presented two small eccentrically shaped dressing units which he called 'Fuji'. Umeda has gone furthest in espousing the Post-Modernist sensibility present in the Memphis shows while, at the same time, retaining many Japanese references in his work. In 1981 his 'Boxing Ring' consisted of a miniature Japanese home with five tatami mats on the floor and low seating on silk cabinets, while his 'Robot' cabinet of the following year, named 'Ginza' after the night-life district in Tokyo, was one of the most startling exhibits of the 1982 show. In 1983 he tried his hand at ceramics as well.

The links between avant-garde Japanese designers and the Italian furniture industry is now fairly strong, with Toshiyuki Kita's 'Wink' chair, manufactured by Cassina,

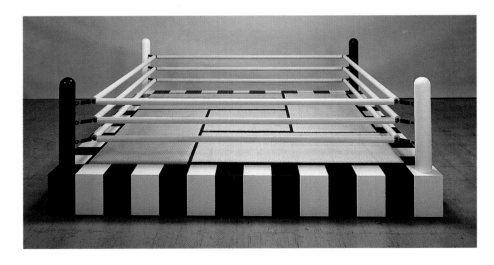

Masanori Umeda, 'Boxing Ring' 1981 In this design for the first Memphis collection, Umeda juxtaposes East and West by combining the serenity of a mini-Japanese interior environment, complete with tatami mats, with the potential violence of the boxing ring or 'tawaraya'.

Toshiyuki Kita, 'Wink' chair 1980 Still working in the context of Italian design, Kita's chair manufactured by Cassina in Milan, with its Mickey Mouse associations, evokes the world of Pop culture which had such an important influence on Japanese design in general.

**Shigeru Uchida, Sofa
1986** Working with his
interior design group
Studio 80, Uchida
produced this elegant
upholstered sofa, the
design of which owes a
great deal to European
Modernism.

**Shigeru Uchida, Chair
1982** This steel chair,
with its classical
proportions, is the most
'Modern' component of
a range of chairs
designed by Uchida.
Other pieces in the
range are Post-Modern
versions of the same
basic design.

providing the best-known example. Always on the lookout
for innovative design, the Italian industry was naturally
drawn to Japanese designers, many of whom had travelled
to Milan to work, hoping to profit from the avant-garde
approach to furniture design in the city. In Japan, too, the
Milanese avant-garde created a stir in the early 1980s,
particularly among the young, fashion-conscious market:

Ettore Sottsass appeared on Japanese television
advertisements and Memphis designs were displayed in
Tokyo shop windows.

The work of the other notable contemporary furniture
designer, Shigeru Uchida, is less influenced by
contemporary Italian ideas and has yet to be exhibited in
Milan. Uchida acknowledges an enormous debt to

Rei Kawakubo, Steel chair 1984 This extremely severe, highly minimal chair was designed by Kawakubo to fit into the stark interiors of her 'Comme des Garçons' international group of neo-Modern fashion shops.

Shigeru Uchida, Two-seater sofa 1986 With their elegant proportions and rigorous composition, Uchida's 'Modern' designs for Studio 80 are exceptional examples of new Japanese furniture. This open-structured seat is made of steel tube.

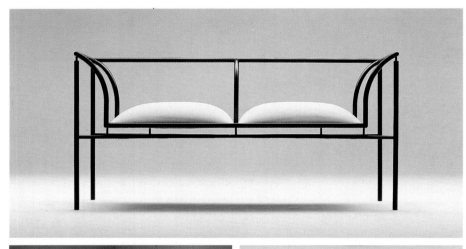

Studio 80, Table 1984 With its terrazzo pedestal, steel supports and glass top, this small side table epitomizes the use of the neo-Modern style in contemporary Japanese furniture.

Shigeru Uchida, Chair 1982 A chair from the same series as the metal chair on page 127, this features a seat and back rail in wood, and corkscrew legs at the front. The overall effect is a much softer, more expressive variation on a theme.

Modernism in his work and claims that the European Modern Movement has been the greatest influence on twentieth-century Japanese design ideals. At the same time, he makes numerous references to traditional Japanese aesthetics, justifying his combination of minimal form with decoration, for example, by reference to their co-existence in Buddhist temples at Nara. Many qualities of his work – among them his concern with craftsmanship and with harmonious composition, and his clear love of materials, both wood and metal – recall traditional Japanese values.

Uchida's chairs cover the spectrum from restrained and classical to effusive and decorative. The simplest items are elegant exercises in geometric composition with round backs, round or square seats and undecorated legs. In others, however, the legs melt into fluid, organic expressive forms or mutate into decorative shapes. Uchida believes that while the seat, backs and arms of a chair are determined by functional requirements, the legs are open to symbolic and aesthetic variation and manipulation. As a result, his chairs are hybrid objects which succeed in combining traditional, Modern and Post-Modern features.

The link between furniture, interior and fashion design is strong in 1980s' Japan. The design group Studio 80, of which Uchida is the president, for example, has worked on striking, minimal interiors for a number of fashion boutiques, among them one for Yohji Yamamoto in New York. Kuramata has also designed shop interiors for Issey Miyake, in Tokyo, Paris and New York. In turn, Rei Kawakubo, the owner of the Comme des Garçons chain of fashion stores, has designed an extremely minimal metal chair which is the perfect complement to the spaces within her highly controlled commercial interiors.

Studio 80, Bushoan interior, Tokyo 1984 Designed by I. Mitsuhashi for Studio 80, this minimal, monochrome interior for a fashion store in Tokyo is typical of the kind of design for which Japan has become so well known in the 1980s. The intention is to turn the space into a kind of gallery and the goods, by implication, into 'art'.

Motomi Kawakami, Table 1985 Of all the contemporary Japanese furniture designers, Kawakami is the one whose work is most surely aligned with the 'craft' aesthetic. Beautifully made and highly finished, this wooden table recalls traditional Japanese craftsmanship.

Motomi Kawakami, 'Blitz' chair 1977 One of Kawakami's earliest designs, produced in 1982, the Blitz folding chair is remarkable for its compactness as well as its visual elegance and simplicity.

Motomi Kawakami, Desk 1986 A highly crafted, beautifully detailed piece of furniture, the aesthetic of this desk owes much to traditional Japanese design.

Furniture is now both big business and high fashion in Japan. Chairs, and other items of furniture, as well as such low-technology 'life-style' objects as clocks, lights and fruit bowls, are now an integral aspect of the new Japanese 'domestic landscape'. Many architects and designers including Masayuki Kurokawa and Shiro Kuramata have produced clock designs with minimal features.

The cultural gap between sophisticated one-off or batch-produced objects like chairs and clocks and the highly complex gadgets emerging from the large corporations – Sony, Sharp, Sanyo and Canon among them – is enormous. These exclusive items descend directly from Japanese craft traditions and recall a time when individual craftsmen made all the appendages of daily life. Their objects performed both ritualistic and utilitarian functions and the craftsman worked, on the basis of long-established traditions at the service of the community. Today the spirit and values of those traditions are retained in the objects produced by contemporary Japanese craftsmen, designers and architects.

Chapter 9

Crafts

Japanese products used to be synonymous with 'craft' and, even in the post-war renaissance of Japanese culture, crafts have played, and continue to play, an important role.

In spite of their firm position within Japanese traditional culture, the Japanese handicrafts – ceramics, metalwork, textiles, lacquerwork, and so on – were under a direct threat from the industrial developments which so dramatically transformed Japan from the 1860s onwards. A lowering of aesthetic standards rather than an elimination of the production of traditional Japanese artefacts was the perceived threat. From the early years of this century attempts were made to ensure both the survival of handicrafts and the maintenance of their traditionally high aesthetic quality. In 1913, the Ministry of Agriculture and Commerce held the first of ten exhibitions aimed at raising the standards of handicrafts and, through the 1920s,

pressure groups – among them the 'Mingei' (folk arts and crafts) movement led by Yanagi Soetsu and the 'folklore' movement established by Yanagida Kunio – were established to promote their role within contemporary Japanese culture.

Not surprisingly, the medium which has done more than any other to bring traditional Japanese aesthetic concepts into the modern world is ceramics. In the hands of such potters as Shoji Hamada and Kentichi Tomimoto many of Japan's earlier cultural achievements have been sustained in modern artefacts. Pottery is one of Japan's oldest industries and has played an important role in daily life, especially in the context of the tea-ceremony, since before the Edo period. In this century it has served to provide a parallel tradition to that of industrial manufacture and to create a focus for the whole handicrafts' movement. Several

Kentichi Tomimoto, White porcelain covered pot Along with Shoji Hamada, Tomimoto is one of the pioneers of the modern Japanese ceramic movement. His contact with Bernard Leach made him known in the West but his work is firmly entrenched within Japanese aesthetic traditions.

Shoji Hamada, Tea bowl, white glaze with iron brushwork Hamada has been the leading voice in the modern Japanese craft movement since the 1920s. His work is both traditional and modern at the same time and he has exerted an enormous influence on young ceramists in the years since 1945.

Shoji Hamada, Square plate This plate with a khaki glaze and characters and motif in red and green shows how deftly Hamada combines simple decorative details with his essentially plain forms.

schools of contemporary pottery which share a commitment to the concept of 'folk art' emerged more or less simultaneously in the 1920s, and their ideals dominated the craft until after the Second World War. Although their work varies in appearance – from the very simple forms of those associated with the Nitten School to the more decorative pieces inspired by traditional Imari and Nabeshima ware – they share this same attitude to the past. Perhaps the best-known of the tradition-inspired work from the years before the Second World War is that of Shoji Hamada, who combined traditional Japanese folk art pottery with English slip-ware (he became acquainted with the latter while working with Bernard Leach in England). Hamada founded the Japanese Craft Movement in 1929 and has done more than any other single individual to promote Japanese crafts in this century.

After the Second World War, in the face of increased mass production, greater efforts were made to sustain the

Tatsuzo Shimaoka, Spouted bowl A piece of modern ceramics, with an inlaid design with fly ash effect, this owes its appearance almost entirely to traditional Japanese aesthetic concepts, particularly 'shibui'.

Takashi Sugimoto, Box in wood and metal This high-quality contemporary Japanese craft work exploits the 'natural' aesthetic of the materials used.

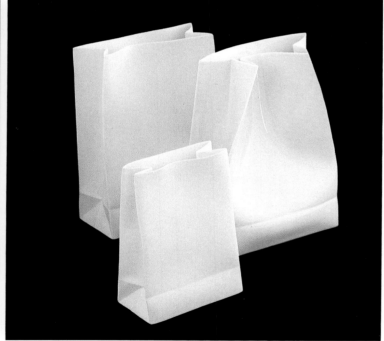

Makoto Komatsu, Crinkle series, Super Bag 1979 Komatsu's delightful 'bag' pots in porcelain combine the Pop concept of the 'found', mass-produced urban object with Japanese craftsmanship.

traditional Japanese crafts, particularly ceramics. One force has been the annual exhibition of contemporary ceramics held by the Asahi Press since 1952. At about the same time as these exhibitions started, the 'Vanguard' school was founded by a group of young potters who wanted to instil new values into the medium. This group, particularly Ko Yamada and Junkichi Kumakara, attempted to find new forms while still retaining traditional standards of craftsmanship. Their work reached its greatest exposure in a major exhibition held in 1968 at the Kyoto Museum.

The influence of craft work has extended far beyond the making of ceramics and has provided an aesthetic model for designers working in industry. In 1956, the same year in which the Japan Pottery Design Centre was formed, the Japanese Designer-Craftsman Association was created.

According to Masaru Katsumie, its president, Yusaku Aida, was primarily concerned with 'the essential function of handicrafts in the mechanical environment of today'.[1] His personal means of achieving this was through the application of ceramic reliefs and decoration to the surfaces of modern buildings. But even where the use of craft features is not so obvious there can be little doubt that it is largely through the continued enthusiasm and support for craft values and traditions in the post-war period that Japan has been able to sustain high aesthetic standards in more industrial products. The attention to visual detail, and the retention of the traditional valuation of quality in the crafts, have served as a model for mass-manufacturing industry.

At the same time as they have exerted an influence on industrial design, the traditional crafts have retained their

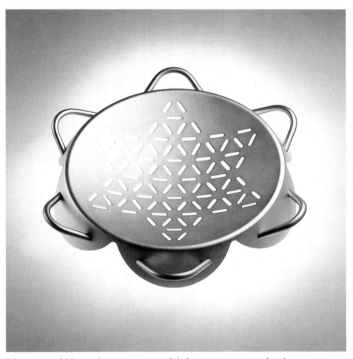

Masanori Umeda, Fruit bowl In addition to his ceramics for Memphis *(see page 124)*, Umeda's forays into craft and design include this aluminium fruit bowl which owes a great deal to the 'Pop' influence of Memphis, while retaining a respect for materials which has its roots in traditional Japanese culture.

Masanori Umeda, Light Another highly contemporary product from the prolific architect, this is not a craft object in a traditional sense. Nonetheless, it owes much to the aesthetic precepts developed in the handicrafts.

T. Nishioka, Desk tidies 1983 These small metal objects, designed for Studio 80, are produced in batches rather than *en masse*, and combine the traditional minimal aesthetic with a contemporary 'high-tech' look.

Masayuki Kurakawa, Rubber clock Kurakawa's clock is a modern version in a new material of an object which has fascinated craftsmen and designers for centuries. The clock has inspired a number of pieces by contemporary Japanese architects and designers – most of them exercises in minimalism. A shop in the Axis building in Tokyo is devoted exclusively to clocks.

Toshimaru Uehara, 'Yui's dream' 1986
While one branch of contemporary Japanese craft can be termed 'design', the other is closer to fine art. Although the imagery in this textile design is modern, it has been executed using traditional techniques.

pre-industrial identities in the years since 1945. This has resulted in strong contemporary pottery, lacquerwork, metalwork and textile movements, some simply perpetuating traditional methods and styles but others using them as a basis for more contemporary, experimental work. In textiles, for example, a number of artists have, in the 1980s, been reviving traditional dyeing and printing techniques associated with the kimono, but using them in new, exciting ways. Most notably Jun Mitsuhashi, Mitsuhiro Shimura and Toshimaru Uehara, have evolved bright, bold, highly contemporary patterns which are entirely dependent upon the skilful appropriation and re-utilization of traditional craft methods. Inevitably their work is closer to fine art than to design.

Many architects and designers have found, in the production of artefacts which fall into the traditional craft categories, an appropriate means of expressing themselves in a world in which barriers between media are being increasingly broken down. Thus, for example, the furniture designer Shigeru Uchida's lacquer bowls are a strong statement about his alliance with traditional craft skills as are product designer Makoto Komatsu's 'packages' in unglazed porcelain, Masanori Umeda's fruit-tray in aluminium and interior designer Takashi Sugimoto's boxes in wood and metal. Extensions of architecture and of industrial design, these objects depend upon traditional crafts for their aesthetic values and the quality of their workmanship.

Conclusion

*'The Japanese have been able to westernize their society
but still preserve a keen sense of their own special identity'*[1]

Design in contemporary Japan is thriving and is one of the major reasons why Japanese goods continue to make such an impact in the West.

The richness of today's Japanese design movement undoubtedly depends on the apparent contradictions it contains. At the same time as it embraces the potential of the most advanced modern technology, in a number of areas it has reverted to a simple, monochrome, almost 'anti-industrial' aesthetic. While recalling the values of traditional Japanese society, in which Buddhist austerity guided every action, it has also taken on board – more visibly perhaps than any other industrialized country – the high level of cultural complexity associated with advanced capitalism and mass consumption. It has revived the tenets of early-twentieth-century Modernism (a movement which Japan influenced enormously), and also embraced international Post-Modernism enthusiastically and on a wider scale than those countries in which it originated. In searching for an essentially national style, Japanese design has achieved internationalism. Finally, these contradictions also extend to designers. They too function within a clear set of dualisms. While in the high-technology industries designers have been integrated into Japan's unique company structure, based on the idea of the extended family, in those areas – fashion, architecture and graphic design – where individuals can and do emerge, Japan has contributed enormously to the international pool of 'designer-superstars'.

These contradictions are not weaknesses, however. They are the life-blood of Japanese design and culture. They are inherent in Japan's continued propensity for eclecticism, in its ability to retain the old while searching for the new, and in the ease with which it functions, simultaneously, on a number of different levels.

The stimuli behind Japan's entering the post-war design race were essentially two-fold. The immediate post-war programme of reconstruction, which focused on the expansion of industries with a high-technology base, was one crucial factor; the other was the emergence of an affluent consumer society, modelled on the Western, in particular the American, example. For this reason, the 'Pop' revolution in art and design, with its roots in mass consumption, found a special welcome in Japan, and proved a turning point in the development of its modern architecture, graphic and fashion design movements. Its impact was also felt in product design (although it took a further decade to penetrate that area).

Today Pop culture, or design as 'life-style', is triumphant in Japan, from the clothes and music which form the accompaniments of its teenage

The simplicity and harmony of this traditional interior – a weaver and dyer's house in Kyoto, dating from 1910 – depends upon modularity, the role of materials and the inclusion of light decorative details to lighten the austerity of the setting.

The minimalism of much environmental design in Japan recalls traditional examples, although now, as the interior of this fashion store by Superpotatoe shows, the materials are often aggressively modern and the context overtly commercial.

population, to the giant cut-outs of Colonel Sanders which stand outside the vast numbers of Kentucky Fried Chicken outlets in Tokyo. Manufacturers have been quick to exploit this trend, producing goods with a strong 'life-style' orientation and introducing extensive marketing programmes aimed in this direction. Designers also, from fashion 'superstar' Rei Kawakubo to Honda's stylists, understand and cater for this prerequisite of contemporary urban culture.

With all these apparent contradictions, the question of how to define the tempting concept of 'Japanese design' remains. The controlling factor behind Japanese material culture is a shared aesthetic awareness, a special visual sensibility which is demonstrated not in a single style but in a range of alternatives from minimal to decorative, from Modern to Post-Modern. In the end, Japan's special talent in design is to borrow first from elsewhere, but then, on the basis of shared cultural traditions, to turn what is borrowed into a new, unique and distinctly Japanese phenomenon. It is this which, in the end, makes Japanese design so rich culturally and so exciting visually.

Bibliography

Books

Adburgham, A. *Libertys: A Biography of a Shop* London 1975

Akimoto, S. *Family Life in Japan* Tokyo 1937

Aslin, E. *The Aesthetic Movement: Prelude to Art Nouveau* London 1981

Banham, R.R. and Suzuki, H. *Contemporary Architecture of Japan 1958-1984* London 1985

Barthes, R. *L'Empire des Signes* Paris 1970

Beard, G. *Modern Ceramics* London 1969

Benedict, R. *The Chrysanthemum and the Sword* London 1967

Boyd, R. *New Directions in Japanese Architecture* New York 1968

Christopher, R.C. *The Japanese Mind* London 1984

Earle, J. (Ed.) *Japanese Art and Design* London 1986

Entwistle, B. *Japan's Decisive Decade* London 1985

Fawcett, C. *The New Japanese House: Ritual and Anti-Ritual Patterns of Dwelling* London 1980

Hamada, S. *Modern Japanese Ceramic Art and Artists* Tokyo 1978

Hidaka, R. *The Price of Affluence: Dilemmas of Contemporary Japan* London 1984

Ike, N. *Japan: The New Superstate* California 1973

Joly, H.L. *Japanese Art and handicraft* London 1976

Kamata, S. *Japan in the Passing Lane* London 1984

Kimura, K. (Ed.) *Package Design in Japan: Its History and Faces* Tokyo 1976

Koren, L. *New Fashion Japan* London 1986

Kurakawa, K. *Metabolism in Architecture* London 1977

Leach, B. *A Potter in Japan* London 1960

Mitsukuni, Y., Ikko, T. and Tsune, S. (Eds) *The Hybrid Culture: What Happened When East and West Met* Tokyo 1984

Miyake, I. *East Meets West* Tokyo 1982

Morita, A. *Made in Japan: Akio Morita and Sony* New York 1986

Morris, J. *Traveller from Tokyo* London 1945

Murgatroyd, K. *Modern Graphics* London 1969

Richards, J.M. *An Architectural Journey in Japan* London 1963

Sadler, A.L. and Tuttle, C.E. *The Japanese Tea-Ceremony* London 1962

Sanders, S. *Honda: The Man and His Machines* Tokyo 1982

Sansom, Sir G.B. *Japan: A Short Cultural History* London 1952

Smolan, R. *A Day in the Life of Japan* London 1986

Storry, R. *A History of Modern Japan* Harmondsworth 1960

Varley, H.P. *Japanese Culture: A Short History* London 1973

Structure of Dexterity: Industrial Design Works in Japan Tokyo 1983

The Hundred Year History of Mitsui and Co. Ltd 1876-1976 Tokyo 1976

Exhibition catalogues

London: Boilerhouse Project *Sony Design* London 1982

London: 9H Gallery *Tadao Ando: Breathing Geometry* Oct/Nov 1986

London: Victoria and Albert Museum *Japan Style* 1980

Milan: *Shiro Kuramata e Cappellini: Progetti Compiuti* Sep 1986

New York: Gallery 91 *Design Message from Japan* Nov 1983

Tokyo: Crafts Gallery, National Museum of Modern Art *Masterpieces of Japanese Crafts* March 1970

Tokyo: Kokuritsu Kindai Bijutsukan *30 Years of Modern Japanese Traditional Crafts* 1983

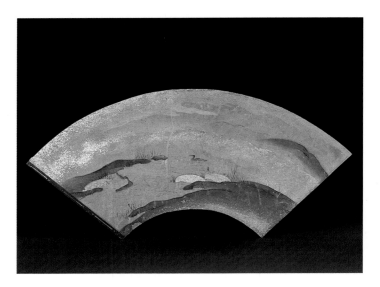

This seventeenth-century fan in the Tosa style is a sharp contrast to the much more ornate examples which captivated Europe in the nineteenth century.

Articles

Alpha, S. 'Kimono Culture' *Crafts* (66) Jan/Feb 1984

Evans, B. 'Design-Style Management, Product Design and Corporate Strategy' *Design Studies* Jan 1985

Fawcett, C. 'Arata Isozaki *Studio International* Jan/Feb 1983

Fukuda, S. 'Katsu Kimura: A Japanese Packaging Magician' *Graphis* 222 Nov/Dec 1982

Ikeda, E. 'Toyota Crown – Design and Character' *Car Styling* (9) Jan 1975

Jencks, C. 'The Pluralism of Recent Japanese Architecture' *RSA Journal* Nov 1979

Kanise, Y. 'The Japanese Way of Typography' *Print* (USA) Sep/Oct 1981

Kato, S. 'Kisho Kurakawa: Philosophy As Built' *Studio International* Jan-Feb 1983

Katsumie, M. 'Where East Meets West' *Designer* May 1973

Kawahara, S. 'Japanese Industry: Design for the Disabled' *Studio International* Jan/Feb 1983

Lorenz, C. 'Why Sony Has Given New Impetus to Design' *Financial Times* 9 Sep 1983

Lucio-Meyer, J.J. de 'Japanese Posters at the Stedelyk' *Penrose Annual* 1977/78

Nakayama, N. 'Graphic Design in Japan 1981' *Graphis* May/June 1982

Polan, B. 'Issey Miyake: Illusionist' *The Fashion Year* London 1983

Popham, P. 'Issey Miyake' *Blueprint* March 1985

Popham, P. 'Sony' *Design* Oct 1981

Ronson, G. 'Japan: The Shock of the New' *The Fashion Year* London 1983

Smith, K. 'Behind the Japanese Miracle' *The British Economic Crisis* Harmondsworth 1984

Sparke, P. 'Contemporary Japanese Furniture' *Interior Designer's Handbook* London 1985

Sudjic, D. 'Rei Kawakubo' *Sunday Times* 20 April 1986

Watanabe, H. 'Kahn and Japan' *Progressive Architecture* Dec 1984

Yamaguchi, J.K. 'Yahama Design' *Car Styling* (19) Summer 1977

Yamamoto, H. 'Japan: Industrial Design Renaissance' *Design* (130) Oct 1959

Yatsuka, H. 'Japanese Architecture after Modernism' *Oppositions* (23) Winter 1981

'Global New Waves in the '80s' *Graphic Design* June 1980

'Hanae Mori: Legend in Her Own time' *American Fabric and Fashion* (100) Spring 1974

'History of Cedric/Gloria' *Car Styling* (12) Oct 1975

'Honda' *Car Styling* (6) April 1974

'Ikko Tanaka' *Graphic Design* Dec 1979

'Issey Miyake' *American Fabric and Fashion* (115) Spring 1979

'Jap' *Vogue* (London) April 1971

'Jap's Coup' *Observer* 22 Oct 1979

'Japanese Graphic Design in the 1970s' *Graphic Design* (75) Sep 1979

'Japanese Industrial Design 1945-1970' *Industrial Art News* (5 Vol. 39) 1972

'Japanese Posters' *Graphic Design* (75) Sep 1979

'Kansai Yamamoto' *Vogue* (London) July 1971

'Kenzo Takada' *Sunday Times Magazine* 18 June 1978

'Michiko and Yuki' *Art and Design* Sep 1985

'New Japanese Architecture' *Progressive Architecture* May 1983

'Nissan' *Car Styling* April 1973

'The Recent Work of Arata Isozaki' *Architectural Record* Oct 1983

'Revised Style Trend of Nissan' *Car Styling* (24) Autumn 1978

'Tadanori Yokoo' *Artforum* Sep 1983

'Toyota' *Car Styling* (5) Jan 1974

Periodicals

Car Styling

Graphic Design

Japan Design Annual

JIDA Yearbooks

Unpublished MA thesis

Evans, S. *The Influence of Japan on the Architecture and Interior Design of Britain and America: 1850 to the Great War* London 1985

A seventeenth-century fan in the Tosa style, this depicts a party of noblemen.

Notes

INTRODUCTION
1   Masahiro Miwa 'The Japanese Awareness of Space' *Process Architecture* June 1983
2   J.V. Earle 'Why Japan?' *Japan Style* London 1980 p.13
3   R. Boyd *New Directions in Japanese Architecture* New York 1968 p.9
4   Op. cit. 2 p.12
5   Op. cit. 2 p.12
6   M. Katsumie 'Japan Style – Yesterday, Today and Tomorrow' *Japan Style* London 1980 p.8
7   A.L. Sadler and C.E. Tuttle *The Japanese Tea Ceremony* London 1962 p.10
8   S. Evans *The Influence of Japan on the Architecture and Interior Design of Britain and America: 1850 to the Great War* (unpublished M.A. thesis) London 1985 p.11
9   Ibid.
10 Op. cit. 2 p.13

CHAPTER 1
1   Y. Mitsukuni *The Hybrid Culture: What Happened When East and West Met?* Tokyo 1984 p.64
2   C. Dresser *The Development of Ornamental Art in the International Exhibition* London 1862 p.9
3   F.L. Wright *An Autobiography* London 1945 p.173
4   Ibid. p.175

CHAPTER 2
1   K. Smith *The British Economic Crisis* Harmondsworth 1984 p.213
2   B. Entwistle *Japan's Decisive Decade* London 1985 p.15
3   Op. cit. 1 p.215
4   N. Ike *Japan: The New Superstate* San Francisco 1974 p.64
5   Ibid. p.27
6   Ibid. p.26
7   M. Katsumie 'Where East meets West' *Designer* London May 1973 p.5
8   Op. cit. 1 p.213

CHAPTER 3
1   B. Entwistle *Japan's Decisive Decade* London 1985 p.92
2   R.C. Christopher *The Japanese Mind* London 1984 p.115
3   Ibid. p.114

CHAPTER 4
1   S. Saunders *Honda: The Man and His Machines* Tokyo 1982 p.86
2   Ibid. p.70
3   *Car Styling* Tokyo no. 19 1977 p.47
4   Ibid. no. 32 October 1980 p.26
5   Ibid. p.27
6   Ibid. p.28
7   Ibid. p.28
8   Ibid. no. 41 January 1983 p.17
9   Ibid. no. 40 October 1982 p.6
10 Ibid. no. 45 January 1984 p.31

CHAPTER 5
1   Walter Gropius 1953
2   C. Jencks 'The Pluralism of Recent Japanese Architecture' *RSA Journal* November 1979 p.743
3   Ibid. p.747
4   C. Fawcett *The New Japanese House* London 1980 p.20
5   T. Ando 'Facing Up to the Crisis in Architecture' *Tadao Ando: Breathing Geometry* London 1986 p.6
6   Op. cit. 1 p.748

CHAPTER 6
1   K. Murgatroyd *Modern Graphics* London 1969
2   M. Katsumie 'Where East Meets West' *Designer* May 1973 p.5
3   Ibid.
4   'Yokoo Tadanori' *Graphic Design* Tokyo no. 97 March 1985 p.32
5   J.J. de Lucio-Meyer 'Japanese Posters at the Stedelyk' *Penrose Annual* 1977/78 p.65
6   Op. cit. 3 p.22

CHAPTER 7
1   L. Koren *New Fashion Japan* London 1986 p.3
2   B. Polan 'Issey Miyake: Illusionist' *The Fashion Year* London 1983 p.57
3   Ibid. p.58
4   Ibid. p.61
5   P. Popham 'Issey Miyake' *Blueprint* March 1985 p.22
6   Ibid. p.23
7   G. Ronson 'Japan: The Shock of the New' *The Fashion Year* London 1983 p.50

CHAPTER 8
1   P. Scarzella *Shiro Kuramata et Cappellini: Projetti Compiuti* Milan 1986 p.1

CHAPTER 9
1   M. Katsumie 'Where East Meets West' *Designer* May 1973 p.4

CONCLUSION
1   R.C. Christopher *The Japanese Mind* London 1984 p.140

Index

● ACKNOWLEDGEMENTS

Acknowledgements

Swallow Publishing would like to thank the following organizations and individuals for their help in the preparation of this book. We apologize to anyone we may have neglected to mention.

Tadao Ando 90, 91; Aram Designs Ltd 123C; Arcaid © Richard Bryant 28, 29; Kiyoshi Awazu 103; BBC Hulton Picture Library 24I, 30; British Museum 21; Cassina Spa 126; Jean-Loup Charmet 32; Comme des Garçons 118, 119, 128T; Design Station 64, 65; ET Archive 10, 20, 25, 26, 27, 34, 35T, 94; Katsuaki Furudate 87TR, 87TL, 88T; Fujica 63BL; Gallery 91/photograph by Masao Ueda 134BR, 136B; Shoji Hamada by permission of Mashiko Sankokan 133; Honda 69, 71B, 72T, 73, 77C, 78C, 78B, 79; Angelo Hornac Photo Library 26; IM International 114L, 115; Yasuhiro Ishimoto 87B; Eiko Ishioka 104, 106, 107B; Keijo Ito 109; Japan Federation of Automobile Manufacturers 66; Japan Industrial Design Promotion Organization 51L, 53B, 55B, 59TL, 62TR, 62TL, 62BR; Japan Information Centre 23, 35B, 36; Japan Olympic Committee 99; Japan Tobacco Corporation 96; Japan Traditional Craft Centre 12; Shozo Kakutani/Yamaya Co Ltd title; Yusaku Kamekura 98, 101R; Motomi Kawakami 130BL, 130BR/photograph by Yoshio Shiratori 130T, 131; Katsu Kimura 105TL, 105TR; Peter Kinnear 15, 152; 134T; Kisho Kurakawa 84BR, 92; Mazda 77B; Meijimura 51, 80; Memphis 125L, 123R, 124TR, 124TL, 124BL, 125T; Michiko/Don Cunningham 121; Jun Mitsubashi 48; Isamu Mitsunaga 46; Issey Miyake 116; Hanae Mori 121; Osamu Murai 89R; Museum of Modern Art, Toyama 107TL, 107TR; National 63R; National Museum of Western Art/photograph by Michio Noguchi 81, 82T; Nissan 67, 68B, 68TL, 70B, 74BL; Keijiro Odera 5; Tomio Ohashi 86B; Olympus 43B; Project M/Makoto Komatsu 134BR; Popperfoto © ENA 4, 44; Quadrant Picture Library 43T, 74BR, 75, 76B, 77T; Radian 58; Rex Features © SIPA-PRESS 49, 111, 112, 113, 114, 116, 117; Peter Roberts 59T; Sharp 22, 24, 39B, 40, 41, 42, 47, 51R, 52, 55T, 57T, 59B, 60BL, 60BR, 63L; Shinkenchiku/photograph by Masao Arai 86T, 88B, 89L/photograph by Yasuhiro Ishimoto 87TL, 87TR; Shiseido 33, 95; Sony Corporation 38, 53T, 54, 56, 60TL, 60TR, 102T; Studio 80 127, 128C, 128BR, 128BL, 136TR/photograph by T. Nacasa and Partners 120, 129; Suntory 102B; Superpotaoe/photograph by Yoshio Shiratori 139R; Suzuki 68TR, 76T; Kanome Takashi 96B, 97; Ikko Tanaka 108; Kenzo Tange 82, 83, 85T, 85, 93; WR Tingey 6, 7, 9, 11, 13T, 18R, 45, 84BL, 105C, 105B/courtesy of Koyoken Yonekura Co. Ltd, 159L; Toshiba 61; Toyota 37, 70T, 71TR, 74T, 78T; Toshimaru Uehara 137; Umeta/photograph by Hiroyuki Hirai 135/photograph by National Museum of Modern Art 125B/photograph by Yoshio Shiratori 124BR, 136TL; Vidocq Photo Library © A. Driver 18L, 35, © Paul Seheult 19; Werner Forman Archive 8, 13B, 14, 16, 17, 140, 141; Yamaha Music Corporation 57B, 72B; Tadanori Yokoo Studios 101, 102L

T = top, B = bottom, L = left, R = right, C = centre, I = inset